The encyclopedia of

Flower Arranging

*Decorating with fresh, dried
and pressed flowers*

Rona Coleman   Sylvia Pepper

THE WELLFLEET PRESS
WELLFLEET

A QUINTET BOOK

Published by Wellfleet Press
110 Enterprise Avenue
Secaucus, New Jersey 07094

ISBN 1-55521-333-2

This book was designed and produced by
Quintet Publishing Limited
6 Blundell Street
London N7 9BH

Art Director: Peter Bridgewater
Designers: Phil Mitton, Michael Orton
Editors: Michael Darton, Dorothea Hall, Nicholas Law
Editorial Assistants: Ray Martin, Fiona St Aubyn
Photographers: Michael Bull, Ian Howes, Trevor Wood

Typeset in Great Britain by
Central Southern Typesetters, Eastbourne and Leaper and
Gard Limited, Bristol
Manufactured in Hong Kong by Regent Publishing
Services Limited
Printed in Hong Kong by Leefung-Asco Printers Limited

Contents

Flower Arranging

Introduction

Flower arranging is an art that anyone can master – and the lovely thing about it is that you can make as much or as little of it as you wish.

You may first have shown an interest in arranging flowers as a child when you used a jam jar from the kitchen to hold a bunch of wild flowers picked from the hedgerows – bluebells, primroses, marsh marigolds – a delicate mixture of colours. And perhaps you were saddened when they wilted and died soon afterwards even in quite deep clear water.

But wild flowers (and others) will last in water if treated properly at the moment of picking. Always bear in mind that you are handling living material, that no two blooms are identical, and that flowers possess a dignity that should never be diminished.

Records indicate that flowers and herbs have been cultivated throughout history, not so much for decoration as for their medicinal properties. However, there are few records of any design techniques earlier than the nineteenth century except in China and Japan.

In the Victorian era printing techniques improved markedly so that many more books were available to the public. There was lively interest in the arts, science and horticulture. Botanists began to travel all over the world, bringing back many new species to enrich the existing indigenous flora.

In keeping with this gracious and expansive way of life, flowers and plants were used to embellish homes and gardens; estate gardeners indulged in an exciting new art form which involved growing and arranging flowers, fruit and exotic plants for special occasions.

Happily now, in the twentieth century, flower arranging is available for everyone's pleasure. This book does not set out to lay down rules and regulations – too many of these can stifle creativity and individuality. Rather, it sets out to guide, to suggest ways of bringing pleasure to oneself and others, and embellishing your home by bringing inside a small segment of nature to provide an ever-changing environment of colour, form and perfume.

Arranging flowers, no matter when or where, will reward you with a lifetime of delight.

Rona M. Coleman

CHAPTER ONE

Equipment and Techniques

A few simple tools are all that one needs to begin
flower arranging. The more specialized items can be added
as you become more adventurous in your design.
Flower arranging need not involve a large investment –
containers, for instance, can usually be found in most homes in
all shapes and sizes. A good pair of flower scissors and secateurs,
a sharp knife, watering can and floral foam are some of the basic
implements discussed in the chapter and are recommended as
valuable aids to technique.

A selection of the correct tools and equipment can help tremendously in flower arranging to build up confidence and prevent frustration. If you start your collection with one or two basic pieces and add others as and when they are needed, or as your skills progress, the initial cost will not be too great. Choose well-designed equipment which should be easy and comfortable to use.

Scissors There are several very good makes now available in varying price ranges. If possible, try one or two for 'grip', and test the weight and balance in your hand. You may like a heavy tool – I prefer a light one. See if there is enough space for the fingers and thumb. Some of the so-called 'flower scissors' have very small rings which imprison your fingers. These are difficult to use and are therefore not recommended.

Shears with long-blades such as those used in the kitchen and by dressmakers, are also very handy for flower arrangers. They are ideal for cutting ribbon, fabric and fine wire. For the very heavy wire stems of some fabric flowers and foliage, you will need small secateurs, and for large woody branches, you will need gardening secateurs.

A sharp knife is an indispensable piece of equipment. It can be used for trimming all kinds of stems, and for pointing the tips so that they can be driven easily into foam. It can also be used for cutting floral foam and for removing thorns from rose stems. This need not cost a lot of money – my favourite is an inexpensive little knife which is light and well-balanced, and, when sheathed, fits conveniently into a pocket or handbag. Moreover it can be finely sharpened to make a really efficient tool.

Floral foam is available in several makes but you should experiment with the various options to find out which one suits your particular needs. There are two distinct types; the green one used for fresh arrangements and the pale brown, dry one used exclusively for dried and fabric flower designs. The brown foam is much more dense and solid and should never be soaked. Conversely, the green variety is not solid enough to hold stems firmly and should not be used dry.

Each type is available in several shapes and sizes. The large brick is made especially for large arrangements while cylinders and squares which are about one-third of a large block in size, are useful for most small or medium-sized designs. One can, of course, cut a large block to the required size, but this will produce a certain amount of unavoidable waste. As each brand of foam varies, it is almost impossible to say precisely how long it will take for a particular size to become saturated. If you are using it for the first time, the following guide will be useful. Put the foam into a bowl or bucket of water and let it sink to the bottom. Allow 30 minutes for small blocks and up to two hours, or longer, for large blocks. Floral foam is a fascinating substance. It is feather-light when dry and really heavy when it is completely saturated. Remember to cut this type of foam after it has been thoroughly soaked. To be certain it has taken in the maximum amount of water, cut right across the block and if the centre is still pale green, then it needs longer soaking.

Flower food is sold either in small packets in powder form or as a liquid essence which must be diluted according to the directions on the bottle. The packets contain enough powder to make about 2 pints of solution. As well as the nourishment, which will noticeably prolong the life of your flowers, the preparation also contains a germ inhibitor specially formulated to keep the water pure. In fact, the manufacturers of some brands advise you not to change the vase water claiming that even summer flowers, such as scabious, larkspur and sweet william, which are renowned for polluting the water, will keep fresh in the solution. Use it for conditioning your flowers before arranging them and also for saturating the foam.

Receptacles It is advisable to keep a few plastic saucers handy which are useful for arranging designs in containers that will not hold water, such as baskets. However, since they have absolutely no decorative appeal, they should be regarded only as receptacles and not containers. They are available in varying sizes, in green, white or black.

Oasis-fix is a dark green, malleable substance similar in texture to Plasticine, a modelling clay. It has a toffee-like appearance which never sets completely hard, but will stick almost any dry surfaces together. It is used extensively for attaching wired flowers to their bases, for securing a receptacle inside another container, and also for fixing candle-cups to vases or candle-sticks. It does not however, adhere safely to glass or highly-glazed surfaces. As Oasis-fix is oil-based, it should not be applied directly to special wood surfaces such as wooden trays, table tops or fruit bowls for example. To prevent these surfaces from becoming stained, first apply a piece of adhesive tape or narrow masking tape, before putting a small amount of fixative on top.

It is a very useful substance for the majority of flower-arranging techniques. It can be bought by the roll and as it is used only in small amounts, a roll may last a very long time and fortunately, does not deteriorate with keeping.

Prongs are made from pale green plastic and have four long pins on to which a block of foam is impaled for greater stability. They are inexpensive and cost very little to buy, and may be attached to the container with Oasis-fix. Remember that the base of the prong and the container must be completely dry. Unless the container is needed for something else, the prong can be left in place after discarding the flowers when it will be ready for the next arrangement. The Oasis-fix will never dry brick-hard, but the longer

the prong is left attached, the firmer it becomes.

Clear adhesive tape may be used for securing the foam to the container, especially for heavy designs, or if the arrangement has to be moved by vehicle. Smaller designs will be sufficiently firm if the foam is simply impaled on a prong, but for gladioli, dahlias, chrysanthemums and in fact, all heavy and long-stemmed flowers, it is important to have the base really firmly anchored. Some flower arrangers use green or white Oasis-tape, but this is visible on the container, whereas clear adhesive tape will allow the colour of the container to show through. Both kinds of tape should be fixed to a completely dry surface.

A watering can is a very useful piece of equipment to have amongst your tools. It is quite indispensable for watering house plants, and also for adding water to flower arrangements when necessary. Even though you may previously have thoroughly soaked the foam and added water initially, there is bound to be some dehydration. As flowers should be taking in water all the time, it is essential that the foam is not allowed to dry out.

A spray is very handy for giving your arrangement a final spray with clear water – obviously when you have spent time and trouble making the design you want it to last as long as possible. In addition to providing water for the stems a daily spray with a mister helps to keep the materials really fresh, especially if the room is warm or during hot weather.

Well-designed equipment helps you to work confidently and calmly. This watering can (*left*) comfortably holds 3 pints (1.5l) of water. The handle is easy to grasp and the flange around the top of the can prevents water from spilling out. The spout is set low so that it does not have to be tipped steeply when watering.

Basic equipment: 1 Well-designed watering can. **2** Packets of long-life powder for fresh flowers. **3** Oasis-fix, an oil-based fixative which can be removed from surfaces with white spirit. **4** Narrow-bladed knife sufficiently long to cut through soaked foam.

5 and **6** Stainless steel scissors and mini-secateurs, which are light, well-balanced and easy to handle. **7** Clear adhesive tape about 3/8 in (10 mm) wide. **8** White vase. **9** Dry foam used for dried and fabric flower arrangements. **10** Large block of green foam

— easily cut when soaked in water or a long-life solution. **11** Small cyclindrical shape of green foam — a convenient size for plastic saucers and small containers. **12** Plastic water spray and mister. **13** Small plastic saucer. **14** Prongs.

The array of special equipment available should not be allowed to curb your enthusiasm for, above all, the flowers themselves are the most important factor in successful flower arranging. None of this equipment is essential to the success of a simple flower design and many arrangers may never use any of it. But as your flower arranging skills improve and your interests widen, there are one or two special pieces of equipment that you may find useful to have 'on the shelf'. It is better to acquire your equipment as you need it and not just because you think you ought to have it.

Ribbons can be an elegant addition to many flower arrangements and gifts so the more colours you have to choose from, the better. The polypropylene or paper ribbon in particular is excellent for decorating bouquets. It is totally water-resistant and can be torn into strips of the required width. Woven ribbon, as opposed to the paper variety, is available in a wide range of colours and widths and is quite water-tolerant.

Pinholders are available in several sizes. They are useful for anchoring Japanese-style designs, and also for securing heavy branches. The illustration shows a pinholder and container made in one piece, which is intended to be placed in or on another base. The gold-spray finish makes it considerably more elegant than a plastic saucer. It is also quite heavy and consequently very stable in use.

Candle-cups are available in gold, black or white. They are small containers specially shaped with a 'foot' that can be fitted into the neck of a bottle or candlestick, or it can be secured to the top of a narrow-necked container.

Colour sprays may be needed now and again to complement a special colour scheme, such as gold, silver and bronze around Christmas-time. Old containers can be quickly revitalized with spray paint and new ones can be 'antiqued' using a

Special Equipment: 1 Roll of water-resistant satin ribbon about 50 yds (47 m) long. **2** Polypropylene ribbon available in 100 yds (94 m) rolls. **3** A combined pinholder and small container. **4** Candle-cups. **5** and **6** Gold spray and colour spray. When using, it is advisable to wear plastic gloves for protection. **7** Clearlife. Two light coats are better than one generous coat. **8** One of several preparations for spraying onto green leaves to make them shine. **9** Floral tape used to cover wires and to seal the stem-end of support wires. **10** Stub wires, which can be bought in a variety of sizes and thicknesses. **11** Fine silver binding wire.

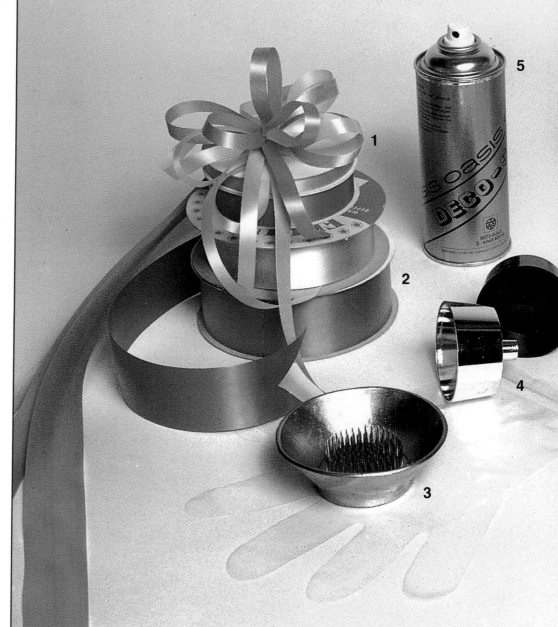

combination of sprays.

Proprietary brand sprays can also be applied to living flowers and foliage, wood, plastic and even candles – to change or enhance their original colours. The sprays, however, should be used on living material with very great care and treated as an expedient rather than a general practice.

Clearlife is a colourless spray which helps to prolong the vase life of some fresh flowers. It prevents them from shattering, and flowers such as larkspur, delphinium, cornflower and eremurus, indeed, any that drop their petals, can be 'held' a little longer with a light spray when the arrangement is completed.

Stub wires are useful for supporting flowers whose stems might become curved as they take up water. *Note:* a wire support should never be used to revitalize a fading flower but rather to control a fresh one. If support is necessary, try to insert the wire either up or down through the centre of the stem. In this way, it will not be visible, and neither will the stem nor the petal formation be punctured, which would cause the material to dehydrate more rapidly.

Fine silver binding wire is used for fashioning ribbon bows, similar to the one illustrated. Make one loop and secure with a twist of silver wire. Make another loop securing it in the same place with the same length of wire. Continue adding loops until the bow is sufficiently full.

A less elaborate bow is made by folding the ribbon into a figure of eight and securing it across the centre with a taped wire. The floral tape will prevent the wire from rusting on to the ribbon, should it get wet, it also helps the wire to 'bite'.

Floral tape is used to cover non-silver wires. There are several varieties obtainable and one should experiment before deciding on any particular brand. It has been known to vary in performance in extreme climates.

Your material will presumably come from either the florist's shop, or the garden, or both. In either case, it will need a certain amount of care and attention before being arranged. This is called conditioning.

Garden flowers can be cut in the early morning or late evening. The moment a stem is severed from the parent plant, its life support is cut off. In order that the flower or foliage can continue to survive we compensate by putting it in water, preferably in a flower food solution. Not even this can give it all the nourishment it was getting from the root system, but it will help to prolong its freshness.

To condition our garden material, before cutting prepare a container of water, adding the correct amount of flower food. A deep plastic bucket is the most useful but it need not be completely filled. It has recently been established that most flowers do not, in effect, require deep water, the ideal depth being about 7 in (20 cm). Bulb-grown flowers are an exception and need only 3-4 in (8-10 cm). As you cut the flowers, strip off any leaves low down on the stems. Always carry them head downwards as this helps to retain any moisture in the stems. Before standing the material in water, use a very sharp knife and trim each stem end to a sharp point. The exposed angle will offer a larger surface to the water than if the stem were cut straight across.

Cutting the stem at the conditioning stage. Stems of garden flowers should be cut at a sharp angle and with a sharp knife before being stood in water.

Any stems carrying thorns, such as roses and some shrubs, should be trimmed, not only for easy handling while you are arranging, but to prevent the thorns from hooking into other flowers. To de-thorn roses, hold your knife blade almost flat against the stem and 'chop' each thorn away. Alternatively, the thorns can be pulled off one by one between finger and thumb but this is a very slow process. Garden roses rarely refuse to take up water. Amongst flowers which may need special attention are lilac, poppies, zinnias and marigolds. Lilac will take up water more readily if most of the foliage is stripped off. It also has very woody stems and prefers to be conditioned in hot water.

Poppies are supposedly very short-lived, but if the stems are instantly plunged into very hot water, or the end is

sealed over a flame, they will last for several days. Their decorative quality is outstanding so special care is well worth the trouble.

Zinnias and large marigolds sometimes droop their heads just below the flower. The stems are hollow and seem incapable of supporting such magnificent flowers. Insert a wire inside the stem until it reaches the flower-head – this will keep it upright and the flower will take up water happily.

Draughts are, apart from the shortage of water, a flower's enemy, so set your material in a cool, draught-free place to rehabilitate before being arranged. Flowers do not really thrive in direct sunlight, particularly where the heat is concentrated through glass. But it is surprising how tolerant they are once they have been properly conditioned.

An appealing, well-balanced design should ideally include both buds and open flowers. However, a fully matured flower does not have as long a vase life as a younger bud or flower. This should be taken into consideration when planning the arrangement. So often the largest flower is set into the heart of a design, and when it fades the arrangement looks empty and disappointing.

Bulb-grown flowers are wonderfully trouble-free, though if they are cut *too* young, that is, if the bud is just too tight, the flower will never develop to its full beauty.

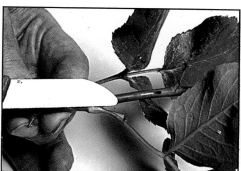

1 To condition and de-thorn roses, take a sharp knife and cut off any leaves which are growing on the lower part of the stem. Remember to work with the knife blade pointing away from the body.

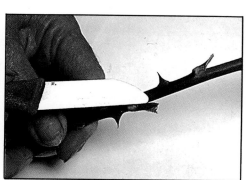

2 With the blade of your knife almost flat against the stem, carefully remove thorns at the base of the stem to give about a 5 in (13 cm) length of stem to hold.

3 With the knife blade at the same angle, and facing away from you, slice the remaining thorns off, finishing at the head.

Two pieces of gypsophila cut from the same branch being treated with a fixative spray (*above*). One of these stems was then placed in a flower food solution, the other in plain water. The benefit gained from the flower food treatment can be seen in the second photograph (*right*) taken a week later.

Flowers should never be cut in full sunshine. The best time is early morning or after sundown.

Material from the flower shop will already have been conditioned but the stems will callous over in transit and should therefore be re-cut. They can then be treated as flowers from the garden although they will not need to stay as long in the conditioning bucket before being arranged.

Most shop flowers will have been several hours, indeed even a few days, in transit during which time they have been without water. However, good conditioning will usually 'set them on their feet again', although some flowers, such as roses, occasionally refuse to take up water. In this case, re-cut the stem and stand the rose in hot water. This will soften the stem tissues and the flower will probably take up water within a few moments. Or, stand it in a carbonated liquid such as fizzy lemonade for example. The 'fizz' will drive the liquid up the stem while the sugar content feeds the flower.

Total immersion is used for most broad leaves. They respond well to being literally 'drowned' for several hours, after which they will last well for many days in the design. Hosta, caladium, dieffenbachia, wild arum, begonia rex, geranium and numerous other flowers benefit from this apparently drastic treatment. Roses that refuse to drink usually revive if totally submerged for several hours.

Heavy wooded stems such as chrysanthemums, branches of trees, flower-ing trees and shrubs should, if possible, be broken at the stem end with your fingers. If the branch is too tough to break this way, cut it with secateurs and condition in very hot water.

The concept of hammering hardwood stems to pulverize the end has been rejected on the basis that the 'fringed' stem that results is an ideal breeding ground for bacteria.

While on the subject of bacteria, it is worth pointing out that diseased materials should never be used and that all the containers you use for either conditioning or arranging should be kept perfectly clean. From time to time, they should be sterilized and cleaned thoroughly. Similarly your tools will also need to be cleaned. The blades of knives and scissors should be polished with steel wool and regularly sharpened.

From the beginning of time, containers must have been some of the first domestic 'implements'. For, apart from weapons, people had to have receptacles in which to carry and store liquid for drinking and, presumably for washing. And what is amazing is that now in the twentieth century, the basic shape is much the same as it was in the days before the Greek and Roman Empires.

To see a contemporary consignment of water and oil jars being unloaded on a busy Greek quayside is to be temporarily transported hundreds of years back in time. How logical in shape these traditional containers are. They are narrow at the neck to prevent evaporation, and at the same time, they are elegantly bulbous (if that is not a contradiction in terms), so that they hold a maximum amount of liquid. Bernard Leach, the father of handmade pottery in England, adopted the classic Greek container as the basis for so many of his designs, which have been copied by his students all over the world.

Flowers have been incorporated into ceremonial occasions in many countries through history. They have also been woven into garlands to grace banquets, used at funerals, and for greeting victorious military leaders on their return. Single flowers in quantity were scattered on the floors of rich citizens' homes as much for their perfume as for their beauty. If flowers were carried, they were usually fashioned into small nosegays, often with the idea of keeping other, less-attractive odours at bay. Hence the word 'nosegay'

Formal arrangements were usually contrived with flowering plants set into large containers. Many of these containers were extremely beautiful and we are fortunate that examples have been preserved in mosaics, paintings and tapestries, in stately homes and museums in many countries. It seems as though these objects were designed purely as art forms. Indeed, many of them are so beautiful in their own right that they were never intended to hold flowers – perhaps one shapely branch or a perfect stem of flowers for some very special occasion.

Until the early nineteenth century, few cut flowers were used in private homes. It was the fashion among the rich to decorate their homes with pictures of flowers, but of course the ordinary people could not afford pictures and so resorted to the real thing. Vases and containers, though not as ornate as those previously mentioned, were still strictly formal. They were deep, so as to hold plenty of water, and wide, which usually resulted in the arrangement either looking sparse or requiring a huge amount of material to fill it. Certain receptacles in the household were regarded as 'flower vases' and as far as we know, no other vessels were pressed into service.

This situation prevailed almost to the end of the nineteenth century, when interior decoration was at its most opulent. But after the First World War, certain values were dramatically changed. Furnishings became more streamlined, due

in no small measure to the lack of domestic help. For many people, this was real liberation – no longer did they have to live with heavy and overbearing 'heirlooms' cluttering small crowded living rooms. Interiors became noticeably less fussy; fabrics were plainer and colours less confused.

Fabrics, wallpaper, furniture and flower vases were produced with a simple handmade style – even then, many of these vases were still too large. Incidentally, the Japanese are expert in designing suitable bases and containers, and some of their smaller ones, with very narrow necks, are perfect for a single flower.

Along with this change in attitude to interior decoration was the upsurge of horticultural interest. However, until the early 1940s containers, certainly in Britain and America, were still somewhat stylized. Other countries led the way, not-

Choosing a Vase: A wide range of vases, in different shapes, sizes and colours, will help to bring variety and interest to your designs. Glass, porcelain, pottery and plastic containers (*left and below*) can all be used effectively.

Do not be afraid of patterned containers such as the porcelain jug below — with care, and thought they can enhance a floral design rather than clash with it.

If unglazed pots are used, a saucer or other suitable receptacle should be placed underneath to protect surfaces from water seepage.

ably Germany, Italy and Japan, with new handmade designs created especially for those people newly interested in flower arranging. Now, many smaller, more logical containers are being produced in great quantities and flower arrangers have a tremendous choice.

Many people have now become more conscious of the innate possibilities of all types of containers, whether they have been specially designed for flowers or not. Indeed, this produces an added challenge since antique shops and the corner 'junk shop' can produce some real treasures in terms of size, shape, finish and general design.

It should be remembered that a collection of vases and containers does not come together overnight, and neither is it a good idea to buy too many at one time. They should be collected exactly as one might collect any other *objets d'art*: slowly and objectively, keeping your eye on local jumble sales and white elephant stalls where you may discover a real beauty. First of all, take a look at the receptacles you already have. Most homes have a selection of bowls, ornamental jars, perhaps a decanter without a stopper, or other silver, brass, wood, glass or pottery containers. Any type of material is suitable providing it is compatible with the flowers. Before you put a container or base into use, do check that it is watertight. If not, do not discard it. It is often quite easy to find a receptacle that does retain water to fit neatly inside. This might be a simple plastic container. Incidentally, the inside of every receptacle should be perfectly clean, as dirt and germs will noticeably shorten the vase life of your arrangement. Many containers can be filled with a strong bleach solution which will do all the work for you.

A container that is interesting in its own right, but far too strong a design for the delicate tolmiea and lily-of-the-valley. The undulating edge and sharp white of the vase's pattern conflict with the gentle curves and softer colouring of the flowers. This shape also poses the problem of masking the foam base.

A sad little collection of flowers (*above*) sunk deep in an awkward shaped container. *Below*: Anemones will arrange themselves quite well, but to expect them to do this in a coffee jar is a little optimistic. *Right*: This vase's narrow neck holds the anemones in a satisfying position.

CHAPTER TWO

Basic Principles

Once you have learned the basic principles of
flower arranging you will be better able to express your own
individual flair and style. But – as with most things – it is
important first to learn the fundamental guidelines.
The information given in the chapter starts by describing
how to anchor your material firmly to a base before you begin
a design. It explains the four geometric forms – horizontal,
vertical, symmetrical and asymmetrical – on which most
arrangements are based, and it describes how to use balance,
proportion, texture and contrast to make a successful and
pleasing arrangement.

Asuccessful flower arrangement depends on how firmly it is anchored to the base. There are several methods of preparing containers and bases; floral foam is now so much a part of the flower arranger's basic equipment that it is difficult to remember how we ever made an arrangement without it. But, efficient though it is, it is certainly not the only way of supporting the material; in fact, some flowers prefer to be directly in water whenever possible. Proteas, in particular, last far longer if they can stand in deep water, while gladioli, although they last quite well when arranged in foam, really prefer to have their stems in water.

Wire mesh, pinholders, moss, sand and cut branches all help to support the material and your choice of method must be dictated by the size and type of design, as well as the material being used.

Many arrangers like to use mesh as well as foam. This is a very valid method, particularly for rather large heavy material. Mesh used alone should be crumpled to fit the shape of the container, preferably with some left well above the rim. If you press it in too low, you will have no support for your lateral stems. Even though it may seem fairly firm, it is advisable to secure it to the rim of the container with adhesive tape or string.

If you are using a container with an extremely high glaze, or made of glass, the

Soaked floral foam will need to be secured to a shallow 'open' base. (*Above and top*: It can be impaled on prongs which have been attached to a plastic saucer by Oasis-fix. Both prongs and container must be clean and dry if the Oasis-fix is to adhere firmly.)

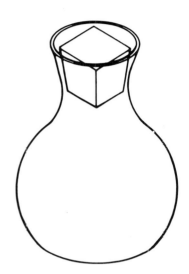

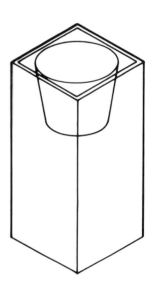

An old-fashioned wire support in a wide-mouthed urn. Both support and urn pose problems: the urn requires a very large number of flowers for a balanced design, and the wire support (superseded by more modern floral foam and mesh) is very difficult to handle. Definitely a container to leave well alone.

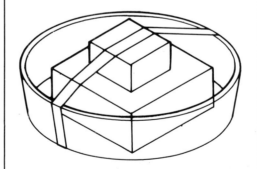

A foam base should stand at least 1in (2 cm) above the rim of your container. Deep bowls may need two pieces of foam stacked to achieve sufficient height. A second smaller piece may be impaled on the first and the two secured firmly to the container with adhesive tape.

It is important to cut soaked foam to a size that will fit securely into the neck of your container. A square piece should be wedged into a round neck and a round piece into a square neck. This ensures a good fit and leaves room for adding more water when necessary.

A large pot of this kind (*right*) and also in the diagram (*far right*) can be made smaller by inserting a smaller pot into its neck. This solves the problem of securing the foam sufficiently well to carry a big design. It also reduces the amount of water — and therefore of additional weight — needed to keep the flowers and foliage fresh.

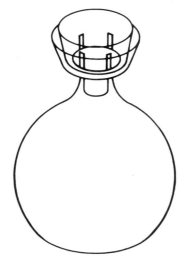

In large containers with narrow necks, candle cups may be inserted to reduce the size, but even the largest cup may be unable to carry sufficient foam for a big design.

Mesh is particularly useful as extra support for heavy designs. It should be fixed to your container with a loop of adhesive tape secured on either side. With a large container, the mesh may need to be secured in three places.

Oasis-fix will not adhere firmly enough. The solution is to fold a piece of tissue or paper kitchen towel and use it as a small non-skid mat for the foam. The block should then be fixed firmly with sellotape.

Sand is sometimes used at the base of a container for dried flowers. But be very careful, for sand is heavy and if too much is used, it could make the base of the vase fall out.

If you are totally without any support mechanism, cut some stems or small branches to the depth of the vase. Almost fill the aperture and they will give the necessary support, though a design with spreading lateral lines would not be practical.

In deciding the size of foam, the main thing to remember is that once you have inserted a stem you have made a hole which obviously weakens the block. If you have never used foam, cut a piece you feel will take every stem comfortably. If your container has a round opening, then choose a square piece of foam, and vice versa. This allows for a better fit and there will be a space left to insert the spout of the watering can for adding more water.

The depth of the foam is easier to estimate. Since most arrangements have some lateral stems, make sure the foam stands at last 1 in (2 cm) above the rim of the container otherwise you will be trying to insert stems into mid-air.

Pinholders of varying sizes are useful for shallow containers. They are very heavy and need no fixative to hold them in position. They can also be used together with wire mesh for larger arrangements that include heavy branches and flowers with large stems, for example, arum lilies. They will also tolerate foam, but much prefer to be directly in water.

Large containers, of course, present a greater challenge than smaller ones. For example, the type of brass container sometimes used in churches becomes impossibly heavy if filled with water, while the neck is often rather small. One solution to the problem is to locate a smaller container that will effectively slot into the neck thus forming a kind of inner lining. Alternatively, a large candle-cup may be used, though even the largest size may not be big enough to hold a piece of foam large enough to support a really large design.

Each time you make an arrangement, try to keep the size of foam used down to a minimum. Although it is far easier to design into a large block, it needs a lot of material to mask it which is, at least, time-consuming. But never make it so small as to risk the foam collapsing. Like many other skills, there are certain guidelines to follow, but eventually, one becomes experienced in what your tools – in this case, the foam – can do for you.

Remember, before you begin a design, to add water to the container as soon as you are satisfied that the base is firm. It is far easier at this stage than when all the material is in place.

In order to travel with a design, it is safer to pour the water out when the arrangement is finished, and take a small can with you to refill the container once it is in place. The well-soaked foam will keep the flowers fresh for many hours but in a warm atmosphere you will get a longer vase life from the flowers if the container is kept filled with water.

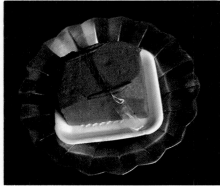

1 Oasis-fix will not adhere well to a highly-glazed surface. A damp tissue placed in the base of this shallow compote will stop floral foam from sliding.

2 The foam, resting on the paper, is fixed with sellotape. The two pieces of stem seen here will prevent the tape from biting into the foam.

3 Here soaked foam has been laid on a polystyrene tray to protect the surface of the silver container. The foam is firmly secured to the tray with sellotape.

4 For display purposes, a damaged leaf can be patched on the underside with a section from another leaf. Use a little glue, plus a little care, to complete the disguise.

For this contemporary free-style arrangement (*left*) a large pinholder is sufficiently heavy to sit firmly in the shallow highly-glazed dish. The decorative stones help to mask the pinholder so that the minimum of foliage is needed. Each stem should be held very close to the pinholder and impaled firmly (*above*).

Each of the four basic forms described here provides a simple geometric structure on which a flower arrangement can be built. The materials you have at hand and where you decide to place your arrangement, will determine the form you choose to work from.

The history of flower arranging dates back to ancient times and all kinds of patterns and forms have evolved through the ages, mainly under the influence of the West and the Far East. The Japanese, for example, have practised the art for well over a thousand years, and they are renowned for their pure classic asymmetrical designs. Books, paintings and mosaics are a valuable historic record – there are the Byzantine floral mosaics in Ravenna with their tall symmetrical designs, the stylized Dutch and Flemish flower paintings of the seventeenth and eighteeneth centuries, and the proliferation of books and magazines on the art of flower arranging in Victorian times. Definite rules of arrangement, however, were established during this century.

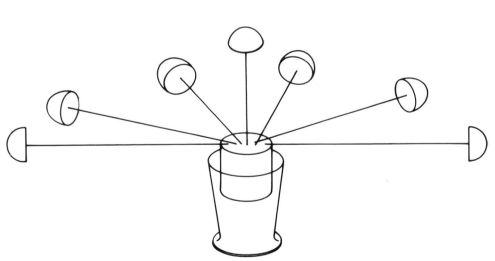

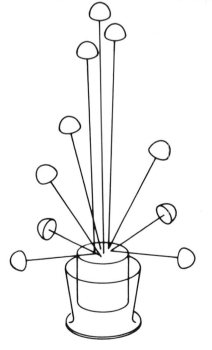

Horizontal arrangement (*above*) of pink carnations, pink bud tulips and gypsophila. One more tulip is needed on the left to complete the symmetrical form.

Vertical design (*top right*) of tall blue iris and yellow double gerbera. To keep their upright form, the gerberas are supported with an inner wire. The method of wiring is explained on page 33.

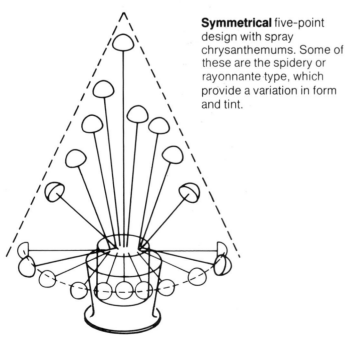

Symmetrical five-point design with spray chrysanthemums. Some of these are the spidery or rayonnante type, which provide a variation in form and tint.

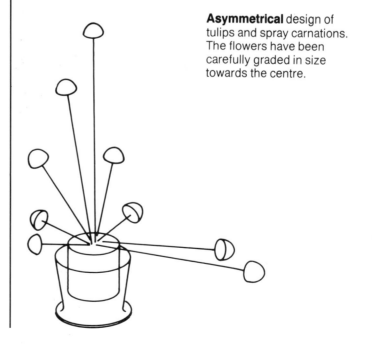

Asymmetrical design of tulips and spray carnations. The flowers have been carefully graded in size towards the centre.

Arrangements with a horizontal emphasis are particularly suitable for table centrepieces where the design should not be so high and bushy that it acts as a hedge between the diners. It is also an excellent style for 'window-dressing' an empty fireplace in summer, or a mantelshelf, particularly in a fairly small room where a tall design might otherwise be overpowering.

While too many rigid rules and regulations applied to what is not only a technical skill but also an art form, can be stultifying to progress, some of the most obvious rules do make sense. For example, most basket shapes would suggest a horizontal arrangement and that the handle should be left free from encompassing foliage so that it is easy to hold. On the other hand, there may be instances where the designer might feel it necessary to place a few tall flowers above the handle. However, in order to break the rules, one must first learn to apply them. To avoid frustration and disappointment, it is better to stick to basics until you feel your designing is becoming more fluid.

Sometimes a flower arranger is invited to place flowers on the church altar, though in some churches this is not

A subtle horizontal design from Korea, composed of pink dahlias, yellow roses and white antirrhinums enlivened with variegated foliage.

allowed. A horizontal design is usually the most suitable and should be kept symmetrical to balance the existing symmetry, and often the simplicity, of other appointments nearby. Having completed the design, always go to the back of the church to check that the central flower is not taller than the cross, which is either on or just behind the altar. It is usual when making a horizontal arrangement to establish the spread of the design first. Fix these two lines first and then decide the height and the depth and work within this framework.

Arrangements for the dining table whether at home or at a banquet are

Carnations, with a frosting of gypsophila. The tulips were added last to give variation of colour, shape and texture.

usually horizontal otherwise no one would be able to see or be seen. The maximum width of such designs is crucial, for there must be ample space for the guests to eat or, in the case of a banquet, speakers' notes and microphones. Graceful and near-symmetrical horizontal designs, sometimes joined with ribbons or ropes of green foliage can effectively enhance what might otherwise be a rather stark dining table. This is one of the many occasions that offers both scope and challenge to any designing enthusiast.

1 To make a horizontal design, first decide on the colour and texture of your design and gather your materials together. Here the yellow and orange of the flowers pick up the colouring of the foliage at the centre.

2 Cut well-soaked floral foam so that it fits the container you have chosen.

3 Not every design need be constructed from the outside inwards. Begin in the middle of this design, masking the foam with foliage and roughly describing the shape intended.

4 Now insert your line flowers.

5 Strengthen the lines with the addition of more flowers, being careful not to overcrowd the arrangement.

This is the purest form of all design. Perfect symmetry or visual balance is present in classical architecture, sculpture, tapestries, medieval paintings and containers, yet few of us are consciously aware of it. Even the word itself suggests grace and elegance.

The technical definition however, is far more mundane meaning that the object should be divided into two parts, both being equal in content. Translated into terms of flower arranging, this does not mean that all designs have to be facing. They can be circular, oval, horizontal or vertical, as long as they can be equally divided. Thus, a design with vertical emphasis may also be symmetrical, or the reverse, for it might quite possibly be asymmetrical and still be vertical.

As few flowers are identical, it is not easy to achieve perfect symmetry with living material. Therefore, an arranger is not expected to measure the two sections exactly for height, width and depth. Your design should rather appear to be symmetrical, giving a satisfying visual balance, bearing in mind, of course, that the basic disciplines should be respected. If your lines are well-placed and the materials carefully chosen, then successful results should follow. A simple arrangement can be made by placing an even number of stems at either side of the central stem.

In choosing the material it is probably easier to get a satisfactory result if you use not more than three types of flower, that is, flowers of differing shapes and sizes, such as delphiniums, roses and spray chrysanthemums. Apart from the type of flower and colour, the classic 'recipe' includes *line* flowers, which are the materials that give gradation, normally with buds and semi-open flowers, plus materials for *emphasis*. These are usually mature blooms, often of a strong, clear colour and shape.

Strong, clear lines are first established (*inset*) for this beautiful symmetrical arrangement of yellow double freesias, darker yellow spray chrysanthemums and purple liatris, with interesting dark green foliage, to emphasize the yellow blooms.

Your choice of colour will naturally play an important role in determining symmetry. You may, in fact, make a design which is entirely symmetrical from the point of view of line, yet if the colour values are off-balance, it will never appear to be symmetrical. Do not let this deter you from making symmetrical arrangements for table centrepieces and display. The style cannot possibly be mastered in one easy lesson, so keep trying out different types of materials during each season of the year. Remember that it is better to begin with a simple design and graduate to more complicated ones as you gain confidence.

For this arrangement the base is first masked with green hellebore (*above*) before the three main lines are set in place (*below*).

Notice (*right*) how the third flower down to the right of centre has been placed so as to avoid too formal an effect.

This form of design is the reverse of the symmetrical type – which is, that each side should be different, possibly in content and certainly from the point of view of line and emphasis.

However, as with the other forms, it needs a firm framework on which to build. So, although the main line may not necessarily be set into the middle of the arrangement, it must be seen to be the main line that runs straight into the centre of the design.

Asymmetrical arrangements can also be set vertically or horizontally, but care should be taken so that they are not confused with free-style designs.

However, try not to become intimidated by too many definitions, rules and regulations. These few pointers are intended to help and not to confuse. When you are making an arrangement, imagine, in essence, that the framework is made up of bare twigs which you will then 'dress' with flowers and foliage. Keep the basic structure simple and well-defined to ensure a successful arrangement.

White jug and flowers in the first stages of preparation (*above*). Foam is wedged into the neck and the main lines are set in place. Notice the small but very definite bud carnations describing the structure.

At the next stage (*above*), existing lines are strengthened with more flowers, and some foliage is inserted. The main lines are now to some extent masked.

Vertical emphasis. Tulips and spray carnations in an elegant vase.

Pink carnations alone would be rather bland, so a little red alstroemeria is added. Notice how the main structure is kept, while at the same time flowers and foliage is added.

A strong structure described with lemon antirrhinums (*left*), which is repeated at varying lengths. Brown spray chrysanthemums at the heart of the design provide variation in colour and form.
Above: A mixed arrangement of freesia, spiced with a few stems of tolmiea and strengthened at the heart with alchemilla foliage.

In flower arranging both balance and proportion, like colour values, are largely a matter for the individual eye. However, one cannot escape the fact that *actual* balance is needed for the design to be stable. It will either balance or fall over – it is as simple as that. It may seem impossible for arrangements to collapse and overbalance, but they do, with very disappointing results. Fortunately there are several technical ways of preventing this.

It may clarify the situation to pin-point one or two problem areas. The first one is the size of the foam block. The size needed is most difficult to resolve since everyone works differently. But before cutting your foam, decide what kind of material you plan to use. If it includes heavy woody stems, or thick stemmed flowers such as gladioli and delphiniums for example, or heavy blooms such as chrysanthemums and dahlias, then you will need a fairly large and deep piece of foam. It should be remembered that every time a stem is driven into a block of foam, it makes a hole exactly the size of the stem. So, if you begin without a clear plan and have to change the position of the stems many times, the block is weakened still further.

In most cases, you may use only one or two chunky stems with quite delicate flowers such as spray carnations, candy-tuft and other lightweight annuals, or even spray chrysanthemums.

In deciding the depth of the foam, you will soon see, with a little experience, when a deeper block is required. For instance, a horizontal arrangement will need more than a vertical design.

When all the foregoing points have been sorted out in your own mind, and really, it only takes a moment or two, your next step is to make absolutely sure that the foam block is going to remain firm in its seating. Where practical, use an Oasis-prong plus adhesive tape wrapped around at least twice. When it comes to tackling the design, it is a good idea, if you are not too sure of your plan, to 'sketch' the lines out on the table with some of the

1 To make a two-tier arrangement First, choose two basketware trays. Loop strong wire off-centre through the larger, bottom one and twist this over a soaked foam block, using small pieces of foliage to protect the edges.

2 Pull the two ends of wire up through the top tray, which will now rest on the foam below, held in place by the wire. Flatten the wire ends.

3 Take a small tin lid and attach it to the top basket tray with Oasis-fix, again off-centre, and fill it with a piece of soaked floral foam.

4 Begin the design by placing the four stems of allium. Insert one stem laterally into the bottom foam block and the others into the top tier block.

5 Insert the foliage into the foam on each level and add the carnation stems and the remaining green material.

6 The completed design (*opposite*), fully exploiting the quality of the allium.

An unimaginative use of four allium (*above*).
They clearly want a little support material,
and the stark stems need some back up.
Adding deep red spray carnations and
foliage in a design on two levels makes a far
more interesting and dramatic use of the
allium.

material. Or, you could even work into an old piece of foam as a practice run.

The pedestal is probably the type of design that gives the most difficulty where actual balance is concerned. This is discussed in connection with church designs elsewhere in the book, but at the risk of being repetitive, begin by placing your material right at the back of the foam. To make it safe, put your point of balance two-thirds towards the back of the foam inserting only a few stems into the front portion.

Visual balance is affected or influenced as much by the colour, size, shape and texture of the material, as the way in which it is used.

One of the best critics of any arrangement is a camera lens, for one's eye can see what one intends it to see, which is not always what is recorded by the camera. So, whenever possible, take pictures of your designs, aiming the lens exactly at the centre of the arrangement. It is not fair on yourself to shoot from either too high or too low for then the result will appear to be off-balance.

This pottery container (*above*) is too deep and too wide for such delicate flowers as sweet-scented freesias. The rough texture of the pot is also too heavy and tends to overpower the flowers.

Right: A solid-looking handmade pot is well suited to these large gerbera, arresting in shape, texture and colour. The pot was prepared with a good-sized block of soaked foam, wedged into its neck and further secured with adhesive tape.

Another way of checking your final design is to leave it, if possible, for 24 hours and then look at it as if seeing it for the first time when your judgement will be sharper.

Proportion should be seen in every aspect of the design, including the materials used, the proportion of the complete design in relation to the container, and the relationship of the chosen design with its environment.

While varying sizes of material can be used to create a good design, they should be selected with care so that they blend together. Thus, an arrangement of gerbera and freesia might be out of proportion. Even the *masking* and *support* foliage can sometimes upset good proportion. When using delicate flowers, such as freesias or Singapore orchids, the foliage should not be too large or heavy from the point of view of colour or texture. However, problems of bad proportion regarding the use of materials are, happily, few and far between. On the other hand, the choice of container is sometimes in error, for it may be too large or too small for the material. This fault is easily corrected by substituting another container.

A well-balanced arrangement of freesias in this chalice type vase (*above left*). But be warned — a wide-mouthed container like this demands many flowers if a satisfying design is to be achieved.

Above: This old-fashioned type of kitchen jar has become very popular and they can be used most successfully to complement modern interiors. The polyanthus are visually heavy enough here, but cowslips are too delicate.

Left: This handmade pot with its 'Celtic' pattern is an excellent choice for dried flowers. However, flower and design are both wrong here — the dried molucella is not only off-balance but too long for the vase.

In flower arranging texture is as important as contrast. It is so easy to get carried away by including so many different textures in a design that in the end it lacks contrast.

In order to get the very best out of your materials, it is important to be aware not only of the individual character of flowers and foliage – their size, shape and colour values – but of their surface textures. Compare for instance, the texture of a rose with a carnation, a gazania with a chrysanthemum, or the shiny leaves of ivy with the dull fronds of grass. This will enable you to contrast rough with smooth, shiny with matt, plain with patterned and so on, to give a finer, more subtle dimension to your designs. It is worth looking out for this type of material and experimenting by contrasting texture with small and large, pointed with blunt or broad with narrow, to give an endless variety to all of your many designs.

Even within one flower there is variation in texture. The anemone-centred spray chrysanthemum, far right, has a knobby centre surrounded by a frill of smooth satiny petals. Like many other flowers, the passion flower, also, has its own built-in texture and contrast. The smooth outer circle of petals with a very fine fringed inner ring in purple, contrasts sharply with the cream.

The sameness of just carnations arranged in a round container as an all-round design (*top*) is spiced with gypsophila (*below*) — to give a softer, fuller effect with pleasing textural contrasts.

An interesting study in colour, line and texture (*right*). Notice how the rough weave of the container has been included in the design, and its low horizontal form balanced against the verticals and curves of the flowers.

All white flowers (*above*), each one different in texture size and shape, can become a challenging exercise. Two or three variations may give just the right balance to a design especially if it is complemented with suitable foliage. The permutations seem almost endless.

It is not easy to find a suitable container for these beautiful smooth anthurium flowers (*left*). Brass echoes the texture and shape and is visually heavy enough to underline the design.

Because communication is easy and people travel more, the interaction of one country on another in the field of flower arranging and also in professional flower design has never been more lively

Obviously, climate affects the availability of material for flower arranging. However, flowers can now be produced in quantity in controlled conditions and shipped world-wide, reaching the public in little more than 48 hours after they have been harvested. There is a vast choice of size, shape and colour; proteas and strelitzias, from Southern Africa, orchids from Australia and Singapore, carnations from the USA and South America, as well as huge quantities of fabric flowers and foliage from Hong Kong and Taiwan. These are only a few varieties that are now within every flower arranger's reach.

Records indicate that flowers and herbs have been cultivated in different countries throughout history not so much for decoration but for their medicinal properties. Thus gardens attached to religious institutions have always been efficiently cultivated, the herbs used as curatives while the vegetables fed the faithful.

The ancient Egyptians, Greeks, and Romans held flowers in high regard and many, such as the peony and lotus, were particularly significant.

But while interest in flower arranging in the West has really only accelerated since the Second World War, it is centuries old in Japan. The earliest known school of design was founded in a Kyoto temple by a Buddhist priest. The *Ikenobo* school has since flourished through 48 direct-line generations and today still specializes in the classic style of *Shoka* – a more modern interpretation of the old *Rikka*. The other two main schools of design in Japan were founded more recently. The *Ottara* school was founded in the nineteenth century and specializes in the *Moribana* style of design which is made in a shallow dish and the *Nagiere* style, which is made in an upright container. The *Sogetsu* school, the youngest of the three, emphasizes the beauty of colour while encouraging the unusual handling of materials. There are now more than 5,000 schools of design in Japan and teachers (flora ambassadors they could be called) have established branches in many other countries.

Returning to the West, there is little record of any design formula before 1940, when an American, J. Gregory-Conway, published his excellent book, *Flowers East-West.* This spells out design concepts which must surely have both enlightened and encouraged flower arrangers all over the world.

In Britain Violet Stevenson has written some very helpful books on flower arrangement in the early 1950s. Her awareness of the design potential of easy-to-grow garden flowers and wild material has, since then, influenced many professional and amateur designers.

Proteas (*left*) growing near Cape Town. These flowers will last for weeks if they are allowed to stand in water and can then be gradually dried, when they will retain their form but, unfortunately, lose some of their colour.
Above: A design from Korea, created for a grand environment. Interestingly, the material chosen — dahlias, astilbe and grasses — can also be found growing in the West.

A Japanese style arrangement (*above*) of three red carnations set vertically, one directly above the other. A few branches of berberis complete this strikingly simple design.

Strelitzias, named after King George III's Queen, are natives of South Africa. Here they are employed in a contemporary free-style arrangement of unusual colouring on a base of driftwood. Never crowd the long-lasting and very decorative strelitzia, and be sure they are really well conditioned.

The Japanese container, with its twisted cane handle, is a crucial part of the design (*above*). Soaked foam has been skewered with a wooden prong which rests across the mouth of the container and holds it in place.

Arrangements are generally best when they are designed with a particular setting in mind.

If not, perfectly acceptable designs can be spoilt by their surroundings or backgrounds. However, this is not always obvious at the time. One way of dealing with this problem is to photograph the display, which will sometimes pinpoint any glaring errors of judgement.

The background colour is a common trap. Some colours will overpower the natural colours of the flower to a depressing degree while others will exaggerate them. Fabric textures will be emphasized and others not, particularly in a camera lens. But we are not speaking only of photographic effects because that is not usually the main purpose of a home arrangement. In any case, the eye does not

sometimes see things with as much clarity as the camera lens: the camera crystallizes the subject from one particular angle, whereas the beholder can move and adjust the subject to suit the eye.

It is advisable to experiment with both material and environment: that which is not pleasing in high summer may well be totally acceptable when the light value is low, or even in artificial light.

An example of parallel form design, suitable for a church or concert hall. Here, the flowers can be seen quite clearly but the shape of the arrangement is lost against the background. The green wall camouflages the foliage, and the broad yellow strip overpowers the parallel effect.

This beautiful arrangement provokes a question of balance and proportion. A tiny occasional table is hardly the correct base for such a large arrangement.

Geraniums can be wonderfully long-lasting flowers, but they will not survive for very long under a 100 watt reading lamp. Lighting can add drama and subtlety to designs, but see that the light source is well away from your flowers.

White and peach-coloured gladioli, carnations in a second shade of peach, yellow eremurus and blue delphiniums are the main ingredients of this very colourful display. It is a great temptation to put it on this wide window sill (*above*) with a beautiful view of the garden as backdrop. But it is a mistake — definition is entirely lost, and the sun shining through the glass will quickly burn the flowers.

It is not the line arrangement that is wrong (*left*), but the background. This warm orange would engulf almost any colour except white and certain complementary purples; and it is a particularly sad choice behind the peach colouring of the carnations and gladioli, which are drained of their subtlety.

The same arrangement placed against an attractive wallpaper (*above*), but the effect is one of contradiction. The wallpaper, in delicate coffee and cream tints, is fighting aggressively with the colourful floral design, and there are no winners.

Left: The plain background is a better choice, but almost every other feature of the positioning is wrong. Crammed between a lamp and a picture, on a narrow mantlepiece, the clear design appears confused and 'busy'; and when the lamp is on the flowers will be burned. A more pleasing setting would be a plain-coloured background with plenty of space around.

CHAPTER THREE

The Influence of Color

To be able to maximize the quality of colour by understanding its tonal values, using them to achieve perspective, and therefore create a harmonious design, plays a crucial part in the success of any flower arrangement. However beautiful and brilliantly coloured your flowers might be, a discordant colour scheme can spoil the best arrangement. The complexities of local colour and their tonal values make fascinating study in themselves, and are even more rewarding when translated into flower arrangements. The following pages explain what tonal values are and how they work so that you are able to get the very best from your floral designs.

It is said that if you want to create a positive impression on your business associates, then have a red wall in your office. It is maintained that this colour will act as a backup to the executive aura. In addition to having a specific total value, each colour is said to have a connotation related to human reaction. Thus red is positive and signifies power. Blue is the most introvert colour and implies faith and sometimes meekness, even timidity. Orange is supposed to suggest pride in the nicest sense of the word, while violet denotes gentleness and piety. Green indicates sympathy and compassion, while white is the very essence of light and signifies purity.

The first step is to clarify the primary colours: they are red, yellow and blue. All other colours are made from these in varying degrees of intensity. The primaries can be mixed to produce secondary colours, for example, blue and red make violet, yellow and blue make green, while yellow mixed with red produces orange. You may wonder what this has to do with flower arranging since we cannot stir a yellow daffodil and a scarlet tulip together in a bowl and produce an orange lily. In flower arrangement it is a question of understanding the values of each colour we use in order to produce the effect we want. For example, a vase with seven scarlet tulips and three pale blue irises would not be at all impressive or interesting, as red is an extrovert dominant colour while blue is receding and gentle. In short, the irises would be totally swamped by the red flowers.

Undoubtedly, colour has a definite effect on our senses, so it is worth remembering that bright, striking effects can be made by using warm colours, such as red, orange and warm yellows (these are the advancing colours), while more soothing and delicate designs can be made by using cooler blue-pinks, mauves, blue and purple (these are the receding colours). Grey foliage can also be used in cooler arrangements.

An arrangement with varying levels of one colour, such as pale pink through

to red, is described as being monochromatic. This category of colour harmony is usually very restful on the eye.

To choose any three neighbouring colours on the colour wheel, for example, from pink through red to mauve, will give you a harmonic colour scheme. In terms of flowers, this type of colour scheme is very pleasing indeed.

For a more striking effect, experi-

Lilac, liatris and berberis in a half-glazed Chinese ginger jar. Notice how the receding colour of the berberis emphasizes the flowers in this radiating design.

ment with complementary colour schemes. These are the colours that are directly opposite each other on the colour wheel, such as violet and yellow, blue and orange or green and scarlet. Do not necessarily choose the basic hue, but try to use

Too much of one type of material can be overwhelming. A vertical arrangement consisting of two varieties of lemon and yellow spray chrysanthemums needs another texture and colour to spice it up.

A 'cottage' arrangement (*above*) in a small mass-produced pottery pedestal. Red anemones, a little mauve honesty and a few brown spidery chrysanthemums are lifted from being too sombre by adding just a few bright yellow spray chrysanthemums.

Left: A contrast of texture is needed in this arrangement of spidery chrysanthemums, which looks slightly ragged and 'thin', without style or substance.

Colour Wheel

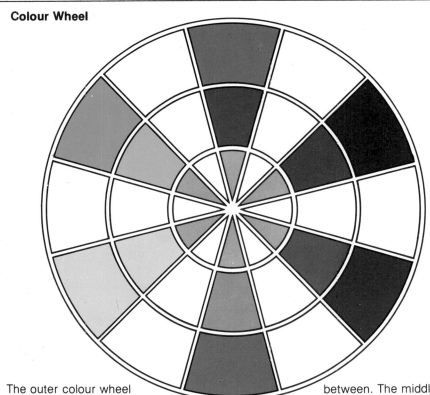

The outer colour wheel shows the three primary colours, yellow, red and blue, from which all others can be made, with secondary colours (pure hues) in between. The middle band shows lighter tints of the same colours and the inner band shows darker shades. The wheel diagrams below illustrate four basic colour schemes.

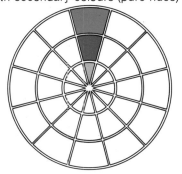

Monochromatic Shades and tints of any one single colour.

Harmonic Groups of any three or four colours lying next to each other.

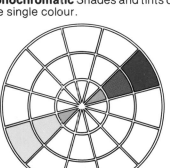

Complementary Colours which lie opposite each other.

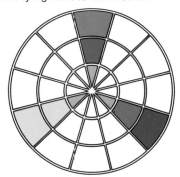

Triadic Any three colours lying at equidistant intervals.

tints and tones of each one. If you use them in well-balanced proportions you will produce very agreeable results.

One point to bear in mind with regard to colour in relation to living flowers is that their colours do change slightly every day. As the flower dehydrates, so the colour drains from it. Some flowers fade more noticeably than others, but in spite of their transient nature, we can enjoy them for as long as they have colour.

Lighting is very important in flower arranging – the colours of both flowers and foliage will look quite different if the arrangement is placed in a dark corner or on a window sill, or if it is seen under different types of electric light. Blue and mauve for instance, lose the crisp, clear colour that natural light gives them and become a rather dull grey under electric light. Fluorescent lighting, on the other hand, will enhance blue though it will make red appear a muddy brown. Tungsten lighting is appropriate for red, orange and yellow.

Daylight and electric light cast different shadows, so if you want your flowers to look their best under electric light, arrange them at a time when your choice of electric light is turned on.

The correct colour, form and texture will also give shape to a design. Colour perspective is built up by graduating and complementing the tonal value of each local colour. Light colours will stand out and become the focal point in your arrangement if you place material of a deeper tonal value behind them. Similarly you can use local colour that has lighter tones to soften and enhance colours that have darker tones.

The subtle use of local colour to create perspective in flower arranging is closely allied to techniques used by artists to give perspective to their paintings. Indeed, the artists of seventeenth- and eighteenth-century Dutch and Flemish flower paintings were instrumental in showing flower arrangers how emphasis and depth could be achieved in this way

Here sharp colour contrasts emphasize the tonal value and details of the carnation.

Contrast between black and white is strong and makes the white flower stand out.

Similar tones of flower and background colours emphasize the yellow in the petals.

This green has a lighter tonal value than the second and creates a nearer image.

Here, the darker tone of green creates depth and the flower also recedes.

Green appears to emphasize the colour and contours of the carnation.

Detail and contrast are reduced because the tonal values are too similar.

The blue background recedes from the vibrant red carnation.

The yellow and red are both advancing colours with similar tonal values.

In flower arranging, harmony is almost as complex as it is in music. And 'that which forms a consistent or agreeable whole' must be our objective. We must not only use flowers and foliage that are in harmony from the point of view of colour, form and texture, but also in respect of the character of the material. Yes, flowers do have character; compare an arum lily with a violet; a daffodil with a rose.

The material must also harmonize with its container and its surroundings. For instance, a severe-line arrangement based in a wonderful silver dish intended as decoration for a brick fireplace in a six-teenth-century country cottage would not be in keeping with the background. A more simple style of design arranged in a copper or basketware container would be more in harmony with these rustic sur-roundings.

But always remember that in flower arranging, as in music, enjoyment of the end-product is the main aim, so do not be worried if your concept of harmony does not agree with other people's.

Magenta spray carnations (*above*) are an agreeable choice for the dull red of this rough-finish brick container, while sprays of honeysuckle blend the two colours together.

A charming old-world jug with a bouquet of anemones on the front (*below*) is the obvious container for these long-stemmed anemones. It is quite a luxury to find these flowers with such long stems, so the design was contrived to use as much of the stem and its natural curve as possible. These are arranged in a block of foam, which fits neatly into the neck of the jug.

This tall container (*above*) makes a lovely base for deep blue/mauve irises, pale mauve honesty flowers and pinky mauve freesias. The straight stems of the irises are set in symmetrically, while the honesty sprays provide a softer outline in contrast.

Left: Cerise spray chrysanthemums, pale pink spray carnations and alstroemeria almost exactly echo the colours of this old-fashioned water jug. The flowers are set in asymmetrical style, with a bold main line following the lip of the jug to the right.

The term contrast, in the art of flower arranging, refers not only to colour, but also to form, texture and the individual character of the material. This means that you could have a design in monochromatic colours combined with contrasting shapes and texture.

Obviously, contrast also refers to colour and how drab life would be without it. But never confuse contrast with discord of any kind. Two synonyms of this word are strife and harsh, neither of which has any place in the flower arranger's dictionary.

In fact, contrast presents a challenge: it is relatively quick and easy to make a small design with one kind of flower in one colour. But as soon as you begin to add other subjects, then you need to evaluate how much, where and, indeed, if. Decisions have to be made all along the line, entirely on your own for, as with colour, no two people will agree one hundred per cent on any given balance of contrast.

An arrangement of antirrhinums in two colours (*right*). Alone, the yellow or pink would be bland, but the longer yellow stems, spiced with a smaller quantity of pink flowers on shorter stems create an agreeable contrast of colour. Rust coloured chrysanthemums complete the design.

Opposite: The vertical design of arum lilies (*left*) is a little unimaginative in this whitemilk glass container, and the texture of the flowers is very similar to the finish of the vase. *Centre*: Add five stems of column stock and a contrast in colour, form and texture is immediately introduced. This may prove too strong a contrast for some tastes, so several heads of lilac are added at the heart of the arrangement, providing a third variation in colour value and texture. *Right*: Close-up of lily and column stock. *Below:* A basket full of contrasts — wild flowers, florsts' flowers and garden flowers. And if the chrysanthemum is regarded as a winter flower, the arrangement is also a contrast of seasons, spanning spring, early summer and winter.

Any material that has been grouped together becomes more significant than if it were scattered.

One of the main points in grouping colours is to know where to place certain colours to give the best effect in both the design and its location. Lighter colours can be used as highlights or focal interest.

while darker colours can be used to give depth, or to accentuate lighter colours. Most colours are usually more lively if they are not grouped too evenly throughout an arrangement. Think of the design as if you were painting it. 'Paint in' one group of material at a time, leaving one or two stems for the finishing touches.

This tall, circular black container (*below*) is a lovely base for the multi-coloured arrangement of liatris, yellow iris, red anemones and yellow broom (cytisus). Notice how the colours of the larger central flowers are echoed around the edges with lighter-weight blooms.

Grouping your colours. Here the main lines or purple are set in position (*above*). They form two distinct groups which are linked together with a single bloom.

The addition of broom and iris echoes and expands the lines of liatris. The iris — a particularly lovely variety called Angel's Wings — is lemon with white-tipped petals, which is less emphatic than plain yellow.

Parallel form (*below*). In this type of grouping the aim is to imitate nature by arranging the material such as it grows. Thus, the taller flowers remain on long stems, while shorter ones are placed exactly as they grow, giving an interesting balance of scale and proportion. The base is usually — as here — a shallow dish-like container, which is packed with foam and topped with fresh moss.

An all-yellow design is given a strong focal point by inserting a few stems of magenta stock into the centre (*above*).

Mono means one, thus a monochromatic arrangement is a design of one colour only. First decide on the colour and then introduce all available tints and shades of the basic colour. Obviously, it is not possible to blend as an artist would mix paint on a palette, but flowers of the same hue and those which are lighter and darker than the chosen colour may be included.

They may be flowers of the same family, but they might also be varied, which would introduce a contrast in texture as well.

Monochromatic harmony is probably the most soothing of all colour

Purple liatris with paler coloured lilac are the main materials used in this monochromatic design. Liatris is used to establish the radiating lines, which are further emphasized by the rich deep purple tones of the foliage. The pale lilac on shorter stems is inserted at the base of the design.

combinations, for the eye and mind are not assailed by possibly conflicting tints. No two people see colour alike and what gives pleasure to one may not please another.

However, arrangements in mono-chromatic harmony – and here the word harmony is particularly appropriate – suggest peace and lack of conflict. Such arrangements are obviously very accept-able in hospitals or in any situation where a calm atmosphere should be preserved. The colour chosen should also be appro-priate to the situation. For example, to take a bouquet of red carnations to some-one who is ill in an attempt 'to cheer him up' will probably have the reverse effect, while deep pink or a soft clover colour might achieve success. Colour is a con-tinually absorbing aspect of flower arranging and every combination pres-ents both its problems and challenges.

Delphiniums are obvious flowers for monochromatic treatment as well as for perpendicular designs. They range from the palest blue to a really rich ultramarine, here underlined by the blue of the glass container. Foliage of contrasting shapes completes the arrangement.

Sometimes foliage is regarded as just a background material. It is, of course, indispensable both for masking the foam support and as a background for the flower arrangement. There are also several types of very distinctive foliage that can be designed without flowers, as mixed foliage arrangements in their own right. I remember a presentation given by an eminent Japanese designer living in Britain who used nothing but foliage in his designs, and yet none of the material was particularly rare. He created many delightful arrangements, some in the Japanese style and some in the Western style.

Foliage should, of course, be selected with as much care as flowers, keeping an eye on colour, shape and texture. There are leaves with a definite blue-grey tint, others with a yellow-cream bias, while some are grey or silver, to mention but a few. Most leaves condition well by being submerged for several hours in clear water. Examples that respond well to this technique are hosta, begonia rex and chlorophytum. Those leaves with a hairy or velvety texture should not be submerged, but should be stood in shallow water. Young leaves are quite charming, with their fresh green shapes, but unfortunately they do not last very long. Some, however, will enjoy being stood in a few inches of quite hot water, to which flower food has been added.

The enormous variety of flowers and foliage that blooms throughout the year, gives ample choice for planning a simple or elaborate arrangement, and for buying flowers to suit your budget.

A contrast in colour and shape, with the graceful feathery grevillea at the centre of this arrangement. A lovely dark red is introduced by the zebrina to the left, which makes an interesting contrast with the yellow/green variegation of peperomia on the right.

The material (*above*) chosen for a green arrangement is not strictly foliage alone since the seed heads of some bluebells have been included to vary texture.

Using these simple materials this arrangement (*right*) has been designed for all-round effect, with grasses forming a central line.

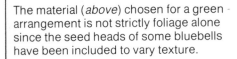

The delicately shaded green and cream vase with its slender neck is an obvious choice for a green arrangement. The bell-like flowers of the tolmiea make an interesting contrast with the deep red fingers of the hellebore leaves and the feathery, downward-curving hedge parsley.

Further contrast has been added at the centre of the design on the left with the addition of hellebore flowers and the still-green flowers of the *Viburnum opulus* or snowball tree.

A third alternative. The hellebore flowers and *Viburnum opulus* have gone, and the deep red of the hellebore foliage is given prominence once more. Below, new contrast is provided with the introduction of four types of variegated leaf.

CHAPTER FOUR

Useful Flowers and Foliage

One of the greatest joys of flower arranging is working
with the rich panoply of flowers, foliage and shrubs that each
season brings. Spring is heralded by colourful stretches of
woodland bluebells and a 'host of golden daffodils'.
Red poppies, cornflowers and the classic red rose are the
hallmarks of summer; autumn is announced by fiery coloured
foliage, feathery pampas grass and colourful cotoneaster, while
Michaelmas daisies, bright red holly berries and poinsettias
begin the season of winter.
This chapter explains fully how and when to cut flowers,
how to display them to their best advantage, and, most
important of all, how to make them last so that your
arrangements can be enjoyed to the full.

Spring flowers offer the flower arranger a fantastic range of materials, including colour, form and size – a complete palette from which to choose, mix, match and harmonize.

In the Northern Hemisphere, the daffodil is the true spring flower and, even though it can often be bought in flower shops well before Christmas, it is still thought of as the signal that winter is almost past. It is also one of the earliest-known flowers. Gerard, the herbalist writes in his first *Herball* of 1599, that Theocritus speaks of a nymphs idyll', describing maidens gathering sweetly-scented wild daffodils and hyacinths (presumably the early bluebell).

Daffodils are probably one of the most popular of flowers, for they are produced commercially in huge quantities out of their natural season, which means that, in cool climates, they can be enjoyed from early December through to March. For many years now daffodils have been sold in fairly tight bud as it was found that the flowers suffered less damage if they were harvested and packed at what is called the 'gooseneck' stage. That is, when the flower has turned downwards ready to show colour. To cut them before this stage would be too early and the flowers would not develop to their true size and beauty. Tulips, irises and freesias are also commercially packed in bud, as are many hybrid lilies such as the lovely orange Enchantment, clear yellow Destiny or Connecticut King, and the beautiful white variety called Juliana. They obviously travel better in bud and will open gradually to give a succession of flowers all on one stem.

If spring flowers are bought fresh from the florist, their conditioning is very simple. As a general rule, all bulb-grown flowers should be stood in only a small amount of water, about 3-4in (8-10 cm), to which flower food has been added. It is not always essential to cut the stems of daffodils, tulips or freesias, as they drink easily, and cutting the stem-end would cause the flower to open more readily.

Anemones, also, prefer a shallow amount of water. Most lilies usually have rather woody stems and these should be cut with a sharp knife before being conditioned in shallow flower-food solution. It is advisable to leave your spring flowers for an hour or so in as cool and dark a place as possible so that the stems can take up plenty of water. This will reward you with healthy-looking blooms and several days' longer vase life.

Tulips like to curve towards the light and frequently this adds movement and interest to a design. But if you want your tulips to stand upright, you may have to insert wires into their stems, taking care not to puncture them. Insert the wire upwards until you feel it come into contact with the seedbox inside the tulip. The flower should then remain nice and stiff. Polyanthus, like daffodils and tulips, look their best when arranged comparatively informally. Unlike most other flowers, they seem to prefer to be packed tightly into the vase. This does not sound like flower arranging at all, but usually when they are used singly, they hang their heads no matter how well they have been conditioned. Garden-grown lilies-of-the-valley are very similar in this respect, preferring to be 'arranged' in a close-packed, handmade bouquet and set into a narrow vase, rather than each stem being put in separately. All flowers enjoy an overhead spray with clear water after being arranged.

Try, whenever possible to use each flower's natural foliage for arranging. Tulips have plenty of leaves, as do irises and violets. Polyanthus leaves will droop unless they have been submerged in water for at least an hour, but after a good 'drowning' they will last just as long as the flowers.

The many beautiful spring-flowering garden shrubs are excellent for large arrangements. Sprays of bright yellow forsythia, delicate prunus, very early-flowering winter jasmine and 'fingers' of witch-hazel on bare branches will all mix happily, either with bulb-grown flowers or by themselves.

Tolmiea

Gerbera

Alyssum

Lily

Nettle (yellow archangel)

Carnation

Lily

Lilac

Iris

An arrangement in yellow and white: daffodils, narcissus and nettles in a crystal goblet bring all the freshness of spring into the living room.

Broom

Anemone

Hellebore

Daffodil

Arum lily

Liatris

Lily-of-the-valley

Japonica (Japanese quince)

Cowslip

Ixia

Anthurium

Freesia

Summer brings an abundance of flowers in many varieties of size, shape and colour. Even if you do not have a garden, you can still plant flowers in window boxes, planters, and hanging baskets. As long as the plants have light, regular watering and feeding, they will reward you with as many blooms as they would in the garden.

It is a joy to be able to pick flowers from the garden, cutting them precisely when you want them and standing them in water before arranging them.

If there is a quantity of one sort, you can make a one-type flower arrangement with emphasis on line and shape. And if there are still too many, then they can be dried gradually for the winter months. If there are many different types of flowers all blooming at once you can mix them together, making sure that the smaller flowers are not overpowered by the larger varieties.

Before cutting the flowers, do remember to have a container with about 5in (13cm of water and flower food ready to put them in. In this way your flowers will last as long as possible. Summer storms can spoil lovely blooms, so sometimes it is better to bring them indoors rather than leave them to be beaten down by wind and rain.

Sedum

Philadelphus

Delphinium

Geranium

Antirrhinum

Molucella

Antirrhinum

Larkspur

Sunflower

Potato flower

A basket is an appropriate container for a mixture of summer flowers and foliage; different colours and textures, shapes and sizes, will all blend happily together. Be sure to condition all the material well. Poppies, for instance, will survive only a day or two, but are lovely while they last. Immediately after cutting, stand them in about 2in (5cm) of almost boiling water and leave them until the water cools. Then add them to the arrangement.

Molucella is used to describe the maximum height and width of the design, while flower stems echo the main lines (*above*).

Summer flowers in a basket(*above*). A plastic saucer is attached to the basket with Oasis-fix and a fairly large piece of foam is impaled in an Oasis-prong in the saucer. Foliage is used to mask the foam.

Grouped flowers balance the foliage and one huge garden rose is set towards the middle of the design (*above*).

Right: The finished arrangement. Strong touches of colour have been added to the main vertical and horizontal lines. Normally, no material should be placed higher than the handle, but the rule is broken here to suit the overall effect of a colourful summer garden.

Rose

Allium

Alchemilla

Pansy

Geranium

Hypericum

Lupin

Strelitzia

Double poppy

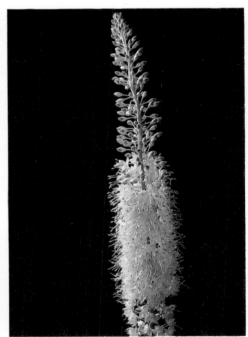

Eremurus

Phlox

Foxglove

Rhododendron

Marigold

Clarkia

Clematis

Candytuft

Cymbidium

Geranium

Single poppy

Candytuft

Sweet pea

Chrysanthemum

Hydrangea

Oriental poppy

Sweet william

Loosestrife

Dianthus

Roses and their sweet-scented perfume epitomize summer. One of the happiest sensations for the keen gardener and flower arranger is picking the first bud of the season and watching it expand.

In his *Herball* of 1599, Gerard observes that although the rose is 'a shrub full of prickles', yet it should not be planted amongst other shrubs but given a place of honour amongst the 'most glorious flowers of the world'.

A magnificent silver wedding gift (*above*). White roses in this elegant silver container make a most impressive design. Arranged in an almost free-style open fan shape with their own foliage, the flowers are set into an inner container to protect the silver.

A colourful display of red, orange and yellow roses (*left*) with a light edging of pale green fern. Notice the contrasting curve of the container.

The rose is not only one of the most beautiful of shrubs, offering a great variety of shapes, colours and sizes, it is also extremely hardy. It will bloom in what seem quite inappropriate situations where lesser flowers might just die.

From the arranger's point of view, roses are particularly adaptable: they are ideal for gifts, bridal bouquets, table centrepieces – and one perfect bud on a gift-wrapped parcel makes it look twice as special. Roses are also suitable for funeral and sympathy tributes and for buttonholes; while for a dedicated flower arranger, the gift of a new variety for the garden makes a wonderful present, for it is hoped that no garden is so well stocked that there is no space for another variety of rose.

Roses also look good in almost any kind of container.

This is the season of mists and mellow fruitfulness, with string beans, blackberries and grapes – hanging thick and black patiently waiting to be made into wine; bright orange Chinese lanterns (physalis), multi-coloured statice and honesty 'moons', and the pinky-mauve fingers of autumn crocus (colchicum), which seem to shoot up when least expected. There are also Michaelmas daisies and dahlias. These are just some of the flowers that provide us with material for autumn arrangements.

The whole dahlia family offers a fantastic choice of colour, shape and size. It includes huge decorative blooms the size of a dinner plate, the medium-sized pompom variety, the spiky cactus type and the really tiny button dahlias which, incidentally, make perfect buttonholes, while the creamy white variety make ideal yet simple bridal bouquets. Even though dahlias, and many other flowers, are circular, a line effect can be achieved by carefully grading the colour and size. Try to use each flower the way it faces naturally and profit by any curving stem that will emphasize your line. Remove most of the foliage, for however much one enjoys leaves, dahlia foliage is not always very decorative and it does need a lot of water. Side buds should be cut off and inserted on their own stems. If left on the main stem, they will quickly droop.

Sedum

Erigeron

Gladiolus

Statice

Below: The warm golden colours of autumn are reflected in this asymmetrical arrangement of yellow cactus and orange and red pompom dahlias. The container, an unusual pottery jug, forms a perfect contrast to the rather busy texture of the flowers. The stems are set in soaked foam and the whole arrangement can be gently lifted out in order to add more water. This should be done frequently since dahlias are greedy drinkers.

Physalis

Cactus and pompom dahlias

Many wild flowers although generally more delicate than garden varieties are undoubtedly worth picking and arranging. They will need careful conditioning, but before that they should be protected from the sun and wind as soon as they are collected. It is the sun and wind that absorb moisture from around the flowers.

So often one sees wild flowers and by the time they can be conditioned they are almost past redemption. It is a good idea to take with you a small knife and several plastic bags, even a jar or two with a little water, whenever possible. A large spray will also help to keep the flowers reasonably fresh until they can have a proper drink. Many wild flowers will respond well to being stood in quite hot water, while foliage and large stems should be submerged for up to 12 hours, after which time they will be quite strong and ready to be arranged.

Plan your wild flower designs in the same way as other garden flowers – picking only those you require. Do not over-pick and remember it is illegal to collect protected species.

A free arrangement of wood-sorrel, speedwells and buttercups in a clear glass jar (*above*). No need for foam here — the flowers are simply grouped and set in the jar to be held in place by its slender neck.

Bluebells (*left*), the delicate spring flowers of the woodlands, can bring a reminder of the countryside into your home.

Vinca major and stitchwort in a handmade pottery vase (*above*). Even when rushed into water as soon as it is cut, vinca will not last more than two days, but is is a lovely colour and looks very appealing in free arrangements of this kind.

Left: A free-style arrangement of wild parsley and a little pale mauve honesty in a basketware base decorated with a piece of contorted willow. A plastic container, prepared with a prong and a piece of soaked foam, is attached to the basketware base with Oasis-fix. The willow branch is attached to the foam by two wire 'legs'. The design is built up using the same technique as for more formal material, establishing one line at a time with a single type of flower.

The soft yellow heads of cowslips (*right*) will add a bright touch to wild flower arrangements in early summer. These flowers are rare in some areas and should not be picked.

The jam jar technique (*above*), and a more carefully considered grouping in a glass ginger jar (*right*). The latter, still fresh and informal, takes very little more time. No foam is required as the neck of the ginger jar is sufficiently slim to hold the material in place.

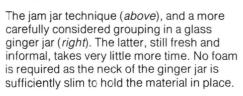

A white variety of the bluebell (*right*) can sometimes be found growing in the wild. Occasionally, too, it can be bought at florists.

The flowers shown opposite now arranged in a basket (*above*). They have been conditioned in a flower food solution, which should be used for all material including wild flowers, making them tolerant of insertion in soaked foam. The foam is attached to prongs in a plastic container, which is secured to the basket base by Oasis-fix. There is no space for water in a shallow container such as this, but if the foam is soaked thoroughly and the block is sprayed daily, the flowers will last well.

Even if you have no garden, you can create several indoor gardens in miniature, designing each one as a cameo. Plants that might never tolerate varying weather conditions will burgeon and flower, even out of season, in homes, offices and shops.

However, plants in general do require light above all else. It is rather tempting to put flowers and plants in places where they will 'add a touch of colour', perhaps in a hallway or in a room well away from the window. They will tolerate such conditions for a short time, but eventually they will become straggly in their vain attempts to get more light, or they may just collapse and die. When in doubt, do enquire at your local garden centre or nursery, or consult one of the many plant books now available.

Plants on their roots arranged in a suitable container are known as 'planted bowls'. The bowl should be large enough for the roots, with a little extra space for them to grow. Strictly speaking, the base at least ought to be non-glazed. If your container is totally glazed, then put more 'crocks' or tiles at the base and water a little less. Try to extract the plant from its original pot neatly, keeping the root system intact. If you have to work indoors, remember to spread some plastic or sheets of newspaper, not only to protect the surroundings, but also to gather up any excess potting compost that can be used on another occasion.

Before you begin, place the plants in the bowl to decide how you want them to look, the tallest plant in the centre or to one side. If there is a trailing plant, this will probably be set towards the edge. Putting a bowl together for visual appeal is not very different from planning a flower arrangement: you have size, shape and form of material, and colour. Consider whether it is going to be a seasonal plant-ing or a longer term design. For exam-ple, a bowl of hyacinths or crocuses will obviously last only while the flowers bloom, but one planted with green plants may last for some years.

Create a dish garden with plants –

An indoor garden in a pottery dish (*top*) with pelargonium, purple streptocarpus, shiny-leaved iresine and ivy foliage. The earth is topped with moss. This is a charming study of complementary reds and greens, excellent contrasting contours and variegated leaves.

1 To make an indoor garden, first lay broken crocks in the base of a container, and add soil and some water. Then begin to build up your design.

2 To add flowers, fix wire or a fine cane to the base of some florist's tubes with adhesive tape, add water and push the tubes into the soil.

3 Give the finished design a final watering. The character of the design can be changed from time to time, and the three stems of antirrhinum, which give extra height in this arrangement, can be replaced by other flowers in season.

usually fairly short-term ones – set in a shallow container. A miniature rock-garden, for example, could be created in this way. So, for comparatively little time and money, anyone can have a colourful indoor garden. A word of warning: it is fine to put your flowering dish garden or planted bowl on the window sill during the winter so that it gets maximum light, but unless you have double glazing, do not leave it there during the night. The cold air will stream down the glass and may have the same effect as a frost.

PLANT SUGGESTIONS

Here are a few suggestions for indoor plants whose foliage will add character to your arrangements. One or two leaves taken carefully from a plant will not materially alter its decorative value, but it is wise to cut carefully, particularly during the winter. Foliage cuts like this will also need good conditioning before being used and most varieties will enjoy being immersed in water for at least four hours.

Asparagus fern Several varieties are both easy to grow and decorative. *Var. sprengeri* throws beautiful long tails.

Chlorophytum The spider plant; not only are the leaves very decorative but the little 'spiders' can be set into the heart of an arrangement to great effect.

Codiaeum or Croton Very colourful and quite strong.

Dieffenbachia picta Known as dumbcane. Be careful not to get the sap near your eyes.

Maranta tricolor The prayer plant.

Begonia rex Extremely decorative and strong; there are several significant varieties.

Euonymus japonicus Will tolerate being planted outside in the south and west of Britain to grow larger and give you more colourful branches.

Ficus radicans Trailing fig; does not bear fruit.

Hedera There are many attractive varieties as well as the dark green hedge ivy that gives you long trails for large designs almost any time of the year.

Hypocyrta glabra The clog plant.

Nephrolepis The Boston fern. A special variety called 'Fluffy ruffles' is really lovely and full of character.

Pellea rotundifolia The button fern.

Peperomia magnoliaefolia Desert privet; leaves are very long lasting.

Phyllitis Hart's tongue fern, fine for emphasis.

Plectranthus Swedish ivy with interesting trails.

Scindapsus aureus You can 'steal' several leaves from a mature plant, which may make all the difference to your arrangement. The leaves have fairly long stems which is another plus.

Synhonium Sometimes known as Nephthytis or the arrowhead plant, its leaves are large and very decorative.

Special Occasions

Half the fun of arranging flowers is to make a design
to celebrate a special occasion, and this is when the flower
arranger's creativity is put to the real test and when it will
be most admired.
The information given on the following pages explains
how to make wedding bouquets, head-dresses and posies,
and how to wrap a gift bouquet. Also included are ideas
for table decorations, hints on how to decorate a prayer book,
flower designs most appropriate for weddings and christenings
and for church decoration.

Table decorations can range from really simple styles, with just a few flowers picked from the garden and put in water, to full-coloured, elaborately shaped confections.

The Victorians greatly favoured the epergne. These branched edifices, often made from silver and crystal, were used to grace their dinner tables. They were lavishly decorated with fruit and flowers, usually from the family's hothouses. Very large tables would have several of these confections, and since the material was not concentrated in one place, it would not inhibit lively, across-the-table conversation. This is one of the main points to bear in mind when making your table decoration. It should not be so big as to block the view nor should it be out of scale with the setting.

1 To make a table centrepiece, mark five lateral points with lily-of-the-valley foliage and mask the foam with molucella and hellebore leaves.

2 Having marked the tallest point with one stem of spray chrysanthemums, cut 5 stems of the same type of chrysanthemum to one length and 15 of the spidery variety.

3 Form the outer edge of the design with 5 of the spidery blooms and place the rest towards the centre to take colour and texture inwards.

4 The finished design (*right*) with single chrysanthemums added between the spidery blooms at the centre, to give a contrast both in tone and texture while using the same type of flower in the same colour.

An unusual centrepiece of fruit and flowers (*right*). At the centre of each layer is a piece of soaked foam on prongs, into which laurel leaves have been inserted with a sharp knife. Before insertion, the leaves, cut with as much stem as possible, were first cleaned with damp absorbent paper, sprayed to give them a sheen and left to dry for a few moments. The flowers for the top of the design were well-conditioned, their stems cut to a sharp angle and the middle ones left on slightly longer stems than the surrounding ones to create the neatly tapered outline.

This charming design in pink and white (*left*) uses carnations and lilies with an edging of gypsophila arranged in an elegant green glass vase.

All brides deserve lovely flowers for their special day. But never be confused by the vast choice of style and colour, for, while the materials will vary considerably from season to season, the basic shapes remain constant. First of all, decide what type of bouquet you would like, and, if possible, plan the colour and shape of the bridesmaids' flowers and any table decorations at the same time. In this way, all the wedding floral decorations will harmonize. Originally, all bouquets were loose natural bunches or tightly-packed nosegays simply tied and held in the hand. In the late eighteenth and early nineteenth centuries they became very large and very heavy. Presumably this was in line with the upsurge of interest in horticulture at the time when many more foliages were available and some brides were almost submerged by cascades of ferns.

However, in the early 1950s, bouquets began to diminish in size and the technique of making them became far more precise and delicate. Many were miniature works of art. Professional designers were able to do this type of work because they had access to better materials – finer wires, different coloured binding tape and ribbons in a multitude of colours, widths and designs.

Even so, the basic form was much the same. That is, flowers on single stems or taped 'stems', built into a design that could comfortably be held in one hand.

A classic shower or waterfall shape is still very popular. It is adaptable to almost any type of flower, is easy to hold and looks elegant.

The semi-crescent design is an extremely graceful bouquet. It is just as effective with simple flowers on their natural stems as with 'special wedding' flowers which have to be wired into trails.

The full-crescent is another popular variation, particularly suitable to accompany brides with long, full-skirted gowns.

Whether the bouquet has ribbon trails or not, it should always be neatly finished at the back with a small bow and a comfortable ribbon handle.

The classic style, unashamedly expensive when made up in lily-of-the-valley, stephanotis and white roses. These are all traditional bridal flowers, but there is no reason why the same shape should not be copied in many other flowers.

1 To wire and tape a hollow-stemmed flower, first cut your stem to the required length and then carefully insert a piece of wire through the stem and centre of the flower.

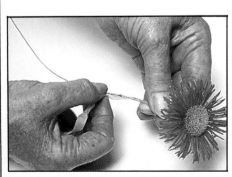

2 Using florist's tape and starting about ¹/₂ in (15mm) up the stem, bind both the stem and wire together and continue binding until they are covered.

A tiny baskette or bascade (*top right*) which is, in effect, two large corsages with very long handles which are covered with ribbon and joined firmly together at the centre.

Top left: A classic style bouquet composed of seven orange gerbera, each of them supported by an internal wire. Five bergenia leaves underline the central point, and three gerbera 'stems' have been added to create an impression of a semi-natural group.

Above: A full-crescent bouquet of spray chrysanthemums, underlined with gold braid loops of varying sizes. The flowers have conveniently hollow stems so that a fine supporting wire can be inserted without damaging the flower.

Two semi-crescent bouquets. *Above*: An all foliage bouquet, which can be made at any season with any type of leaf that will tolerate being carefully wired and left out of water for several hours. A foliage bouquet can appear rather flat unless something with volume, such as the green flower head here, is included.

Right: Green cymbidium orchids and foliage. Each leaf is wired separately, taped and then built into trails.

All the flowers are on their natural stems in this hand posy so that it can be placed in water. To make the posy, take three strips of tulle, one shorter than the other two, and gather them on wire to form circles. Place a few flowers inside the smallest frill and pull the wire tight (though not so tight that the stems break). Then, randomly position flowers around it, gather the second frill around the bunch and pull the wire tight. Position the remaining flowers followed by the third frill. Pull this last wire tight and add ribbon trimming.

The bridal bouquet will, of course, be lovely: the bridesmaids and flower girls complete the wedding picture. Happily, there is a wide selection of flowers and designs for them to choose from.

Bascades resemble baskets of flowers (although they are actually designed like small bouquets with a ribboned handle), and they can be copied in any size to suit both child attendants and taller bridesmaids. A head-dress to match, in either real or fabric flowers, completes the effect.

Pomanders (floral balls) can also be

designed in several sizes. The ribbon handle is, of course, graded in length according to the height of the bridesmaid. Both these and the bascades are popular with the younger attendants as they can be swung around without damaging the flowers! Sometimes a wedding ceremony can prove a bit overwhelming for young bridesmaids.

For a country wedding, pomanders made with wild flowers such as marguerites (moon daisies) would look absolutely enchanting. Or maybe the bridesmaids would prefer to carry natural posies of mixed flowers. If the flowers seem limp after the wedding, immerse the bouquet completely in cold water overnight. They will, no doubt, revive and last for several more days.

Left: A sandalwood fan decorated with a small corsage of green Singapore orchids.
Above: A floral pomander made of tiny tulle bows decorated with a fresh flower spray.

Stitching and wiring ivy: Ivy is very long-lasting, so naturally it is quite popular for bridal designs. Every single leaf must be stitched with a fine silver wire and each 'stem' neatly bound with florist's tape. The tape is not only used for a neat finish, but to seal the base of the leaf or flower stem, thus keeping in any moisture and consequently helping material to last a little longer.

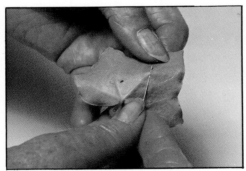

1 Select a sufficient number of clean, well-shaped leaves. Using a needle threaded with fine silver wire, make a small stitch at the centre back of an ivy leaf.

2 Carefully pull the wire thread through and, keeping the wire loop quite loose, lay one end down the side of the ivy stem and wind the other round both of them.

3 Next, starting at the base of the leaf, begin to bind the wire and ivy stem together with florist's tape.

4 Continue binding the wire 'stem' with florist's tape until your stem is the required length.

5 Several 'stems' of ivy can now be bound together and assembled into trails. These can be shaped to form part of your wedding bouquet.

Instead of the traditional wedding bouquet, some brides prefer to carry a white bible or prayer book, with a small spray of flowers attached.

In effect, the spray follows the same kind of design as a bouquet and should be made in proportion to the size of the book. If it is too large, the whole effect is lost.

Ribbon markers are a matter for personal preference. One is usually passed through the page at the beginning of the Marriage Service and the other across the inside of the cover. These ribbons can look very attractive either left plain or decorated with tiny fresh flower heads.

For a summer country wedding, flower-decorated parasols would make charming accessories for the bridesmaids. They are quite lightweight to carry and can be closed for the ceremony. This should have no effect on the flower trimming providing it is done carefully. It is, of course, advisable to let your florist know that you would like the parasol to be used both open and closed and then the trimming can be arranged accordingly.

This classic head-dress (*right*) is attached to a small hair comb. You can secure it with silver wire or with clear adhesive.

Whenever possible match head-dresses with bouquets and posies. This is particularly effective with a period design as shown in the Victorian posy and head-dress (*left and right*). The bridesmaid's posy and circlet are made of fabric flowers. The circlet is secured to the hair with hair grips (bobby pins).

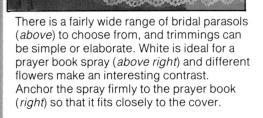

There is a fairly wide range of bridal parasols (*above*) to choose from, and trimmings can be simple or elaborate. White is ideal for a prayer book spray (*above right*) and different flowers make an interesting contrast. Anchor the spray firmly to the prayer book (*right*) so that it fits closely to the cover.

If possible, the bridal cake top should match, or at least blend with, some of the flowers in the bridal bouquet. If the bouquet is made with large flowers, such as red roses, then obviously this is not feasible, but sometimes a flower can be diminished by using just a few petals and joining them in small trails as mini-flowers.

You could even place a favourite vase on top of the cake and create a design on natural stems if the flowers are suitable. The cake top design should be kept as delicate as possible and in proportion to the size and height of the cake.

Decorating the bridal car can also contribute to the festivity of the occasion. The Oasis company has produced a suction base called an auto-corso which can be arranged in exactly the same manner as a horizontal-style flower arrangement. There can be no damage to coachwork as the base is rubber. The decoration can be fixed either to one wing, or to the bonnet, attached to water-resistant ribbons stretched from either side of the windshield. Decidedly a fun addition to the bridal flowers.

Horizontal-style flower arrangement for the wedding car (*below*) built on an 'auto-corso' base.

The auto-corso has a suction base (*above*) on which soaked foam is secured (*left*).

The cake top (*above*) is designed to match the all-white classic bouquet on page 92. Built in accordance with the five-point motif, all the wire 'stems' are bound at one point and then bound together to form one stem that neatly fits into the silver vase.

A two-tier cake with a small top decoration in fabric freesias and tiny daffodils, further emphasized by trailing ribbons and bows held at the four corners of the base.
The detail of the decoration (*left*) shows ribbon bows with a single daffodil simply arranged at each corner.

A christening is yet another happy occasion made more festive with plenty of flowers. What better first gift could a child have than to be surrounded by loving family and flowers?

As well as a pedestal design – or several if the church is large enough – you could have ceremonial brass candlestands which look lovely when specially dressed for the day.

Use long-lasting flowers, if possible, rather than delicate varieties, and make sure your foam is well soaked because sometimes it is not practical to fix a container to the stand. There is generally a small rim around the candle, presumably to catch the wax; but it is sometimes possible to fit pieces of floral foam to both sides of the candle. It is advisable to seek permission from whoever is in charge before doing this, however.

Nowadays christenings are conducted within the framework of a church service, not as isolated services. This means, of course, that not only the immediate family but everyone else can enjoy the extra special flower decorations.

Do try to check them a day or so afterwards; nothing looks worse than special arrangements that are fading. No doubt the pedestals and vase designs will last, but try to ensure that everything else is cleaned up and tidied away as soon as it is past its best.

1 To decorate a cradle (available from the florist in a choice of pink, blue or white), fix a flat disc of soaked floral foam to a prong set in the cradle. A second round of foam will be needed to achieve the right height, which should be impaled on the first one with fine cane.
2 Define the basic shape with white ixia and cream altroemeria. Insert the stems laterally.
3 Add five stems of freesia and a pink ribbon to finish.

Left: White longiflorum lilies, white spray single chrysanthemums and some shapely sprays of white broom dress the Christening candle. Add a white ribbon for this very special occasion.

A simple three-point design with long-stemmed, yellow and white lilies (*left*). Delicate, drooping yellow fronds fill the central area.

Above: For a more special and festive effect gypsophila may be added. This is the same arrangement with a lavish quantity added.

It is quite a responsibility as well as a pleasure to arrange flowers for a particular church festival: Easter, Harvest Festival, Christmas or a wedding.

After the weeks of Lent with no flowers at all, the church can be decorated for Easter as lavishly as time, material and money will permit. Daffodils are usually in abundance together with the new foliage. Many couples who marry at Easter have an extra lovely setting for their wedding.

Lilies are the traditional Easter flower and some churches prefer arums. These certainly are beautiful but are not easy to arrange because of their broad stems. Fortunately, though, they are entirely tolerant of being arranged in foam, providing it is possible to add more water to the container every alternate day or so.

The longiflorum and regale varieties have thinner, more woody stems and are much easier to arrange. They last just as well and also tolerate being arranged in foam providing the water level can be checked from time to time. These lilies are usually transported when they are very young, before the flowers open, to prevent them from being damaged. So buy them at least by the beginning of Easter week so that they can develop and show some bloom (as opposed to green buds) by the time you want to arrange them.

The Paschal candle, decorated with beautiful arum lilies for Eastertide. Notice the candle gives height to this classic design.

1 To make a church decoration, choose a deep bowl and fill it with foam. The second part-block is attached with adhesive tape. Use pieces of stem to prevent tape from cutting into the foam.

2 For such a large design, add a third smaller block of foam to the base, again setting stems in position to protect the foam, and securing it firmly with tape.

3 Insert the main lines of this three-point design first, well back in the foam. The side view shows these first stems in place, leaving the centre of the foam clear.

4 Add more stems, still as far back in the block as possible. See that they do not 'march forward' as this picture indicates, since this will result in a stodgy-looking effect and may upset the balance as well.

5 The completed design of daisies, lilies and broom. A classic example of a well proportioned design of white with a softening of yellow.

Bouquets wrapped in clear cellophane with bright, richly looped bows suggest glamour, success, honour and royal occasions. To add such a touch of glamour to a bouquet of flowers from your own garden or from the florist is not difficult and is worth the effort.

You will need cellophane paper, a generous length of water-resistant ribbon and a staple gun. If you can plan ahead, it is well worth having an idea of the colour combination you want in your bouquet before you choose the ribbon, and you can then either match one of your colours or perhaps pick a ribbon that makes a strong contrast. Follow the instructions (*right*) and you will be able to add a touch of luxury to a gift of flowers.

1

1 To wrap a gift bouquet, first make sure that all stems of both flowers and foliage are clean and free from thorns or odd leaves. Then arrange the flowers and foliage as attractively as possible, longer stems to the back, keeping the shorter ones to the front. Try not to cut stems any shorter than absolutely necessary.

2 Tie the bouquet together at a comfortable tying point with a multi-loop bow of water-resistant ribbon, which has been tied across the centre with a fairly long piece of the same ribbon. It is a good idea to prepare the ribbon at the start. The bouquet should then be laid on the cellophane leaving enough paper to wrap the stems at the bottom and to fold over the flower heads.

2

The diagram shows the bouquet tied with ribbon and lying on cellophane paper. The arrows indicate how the paper should be folded over the stems and flower heads and tucked underneath the bow. The curved black arrows show how the ties should first be crossed at the back before the final bow is made at the front.

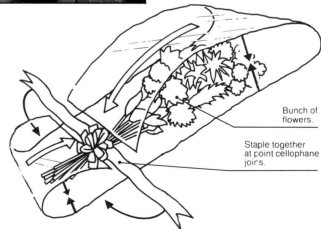

Bunch of flowers.

Staple together at point cellophane joins.

3 Arrange the cellophane over the flowers and stems so that the ends meet at the tying point. (About twice the length is enough.)
4 Then staple once each side at the tying point, keeping the cross ties outside the paper.
5 Cross the ties at the back and bring around to the front, finishing off with another bow across the centre of the first bow. Staple the edges at least twice, but to prevent the inside from steaming up, be careful not to overseal.

The finished gift bouquet of mixed garden flowers wrapped in cellophone paper and tied with a bright, contrasting bow.

Flowers make welcome gifts for wedding anniversaries, and it is worth taking trouble with decorative centrepieces for anniversary parties.

For this Golden Wedding arrangement, you will need to buy candles and several yards of net. Be generous with the net so that the pleating on each layer can be deep and the finished effect full. You will also need three circles of soaked foam of different sizes, and these should, if possible, be foam and polystyrene posy pads, which can be cut to the diameter you require. Gold spray will be needed to spray the candles, net and foam. The base is made from ½in (15mm) thick wood or cardboard, covered with gold paper.

The all-round point method is used for inserting the flowers, with seven points for the first layer, five for the second and three for the top.

Fifth wedding anniversary gift (*above*). An outsize wooden spoon and fork decorated with a large spray of green Singapore orchids and hellebore seedheads, which are tied with nut-brown and pale brown ribbon.

1 If you cannot buy gold candles, any colour can be sprayed with gold paint. Remember to spray well away from the flowers.

2 The candles should be fitted with wire 'legs' and inserted in the top layer of foam. Pin a strip of gold paper or ribbon around the foam.

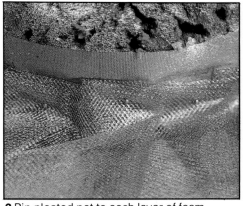

3 Pin pleated net to each layer of foam, attaching it to the covered base, and then spray with gold paint.

4 Insert mixed foliage and flowers in the first layer, using the all-round point method. Remember that all the material in the first stage is set in laterally.

5 Insert flowers and foliage into second layer, keeping the stems shorter to maintain the cone effect. Fix them firmly in place.

6 Do the same with the third layer, inserting the candles and finishing off the top with more flowers arranged to form the point of the cone.

ANNIVERSARIES

Most people will probably know that 25 years of marriage means a Silver Wedding anniversary, 40 years a Ruby celebration, and 50 years a Golden Wedding. All are milestones that should be marked with flowers and other appropriate gifts, and you may also wish to do the same for the ones in between.

1st: Paper	14th: Ivory
2nd: Cotton	15th: Crystal
3rd: Leather	20th: China
4th: Flowers	25th: Silver
5th: Wood	30th: Pearl
6th: Candy	35th: Coral
7th: Wool	40th: Ruby
8th: Pottery	45th: Sapphire
9th: Willow	50th: Gold
10th: Tin	55th: Emerald
11th: Steel	60th: Diamond
12th: Silk	70th: Platinum

7 Completed design for a Golden Wedding party.

FLOWER ARRANGING

For many types of flowers, a basket would seem to be the natural container to choose. They are traditional containers, and have for centuries been used all over the world, for carrying such things as bricks, food, clothing, wood, indeed, all things domestic. Now they are designed specifically for flowers, and are available in a vast range of shapes and sizes from huge curved display baskets to shallow 'Nell Gwyn' shapes, all woven in beautiful natural colours. Wicker and cane can of course be spray-painted to match or complement the arranged flowers and the ribbon for the handle and bows.

They provide endless possibilities for decoration. The materials used to make baskets seem to look right almost anywhere as there is no really strong colour to conflict with existing interior decor. In addition to large arrangements for wedding parties, smaller arrangements can be carried by bridesmaids. They are also suitable for presentation to a visiting dignitary, for example, or for sending to a sick friend in hospital, where the flowers, if properly conditioned, will remain fresh for several days.

Perhaps a special gift might be included with the flowers such as fruit for someone in hospital, a few plants for a keen gardener, an Easter egg, or a bottle of perfume. Even if gift-wrapped separately, none of these would seem half so glamorous as when they are included in a basket of flowers.

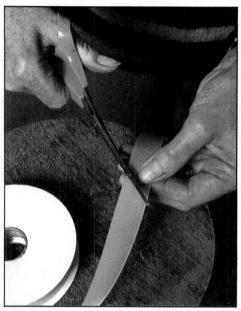

1 To prepare a basket, choose a ribbon that will harmonise with your proposed design and cut a generous length for binding the basket's handle (about 2-3 times the length will be sufficient).

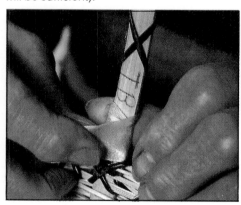

2 Attach the ribbon securely to the base of the handle with adhesive tape and begin binding.

3 To ensure that the binding does not slip after completion, keep the ribbon pulled taut as you wind. When the handle is covered, secure the end with adhesive tape.

4 With a length of the same coloured ribbon, make a multi-looped bow, keeping the ends long for tying on to the basket.

5 Bind the ends of the ribbon round the centre of the bow and basket handle and tie firmly.

6 Now attach a prong to the inner plastic container with Oasis-fix and place two generous pieces of Oasis-fix on the base of the container.

A shallow basket filled with flowers of a variety of colours. The contrasting wicker handle is interesting enough without the addition of ribbon and would, in any case, prove difficult to bind neatly.

7 Attach the container to the basket. The whole base will be much firmer if you can now leave it to harden for at least a few hours before beginning your design.

9 Surround the base with a bed of moss, neatly masking the base sides.

11 Begin by inserting yellow tulips, which have been chosen as line flowers. Place tulip buds low down on the basket, placing the well-opened flowers in the middle of the arrangement.

8 Impale a soaked foam block on the prongs. this may be sufficient to hold your design, but if the flowers are heavy or the basket is to be transported, secure firmly with more layers of adhesive tape.

10 Next, take the flowers, remembering to cut the stems to a very sharp point so that they drive crisply into the foam.

12 The insertion of the tulips is now completed. Add some foliage, including both tulip and daffodil leaves, between the flowers as a background for the next selection of flowers. (*continued*)

13 Insert ten daffodils to echo the main lines and establish the height of the arrangement.

14 Position the daffodils so that the angle of each head forms a series of flowing lines around the basket edge.

15 Add small groups of gypsophila stems to fill the spaces between the flowers.

16 The completed basket (*right*) to which red alstroemeria has been added to give colour and character to the design.

Blue candle (*above*) with silver foliage and sprigs of living holly on a cut section of wood. The dry foam can be glued to the wood.

Traditional red and gold (*above*) for an all-round design inserted into a block of polystyrene.

To make a door wreath (*above*), the material is bound to a metal hoop with thin wire.

Right: An unusual door wreath designed by a student at a German horticultural college and labelled as in the 'English style'. It is built on a wire base and tapered at each side. The material includes juniper, box, various artificial fruits and nuts, and red ribbon.

Christmas celebrations as we know them today are based on nineteenth-century tradition. They are now so much a part of our life-style that it is difficult to realize that the tree with its trimmings and decorations, candles, cones and fruits, foliage, baubles and glitter, have been in fashion for a little over a hundred years.

The evergreen Christmas tree is the symbol of life and survival. It symbolises the changing of the seasons; its roots, flowers and fruit forming a continual life-cycle.

Candles are also symbolical of life, but in a less infinite way; that is, the lighted candle burns to its end in less than one day. Those countries that celebrate Christmas during the coldest and darkest time of year have good reason to enjoy the Christmas tradition, particularly since it is so near the shortest day which is another reason to enjoy preparing for the festivities; unfortunately, candles nowadays are substituted for winking electric lights, and the traditional fruits and nuts for glass baubles.

The door wreath is also a symbol of the continual progression of life throughout the year. It bestows a spirit of welcome to the visitor and indicates that the family is at home and looking forward to celebrating together.

Gold and silver glitter are rooted in tradition, for gold and silver were used only on special occasions. In some countries the tradition of using only real foliage for decoration is still clung to, while in many others, homes are decorated with artificial foliage or glittered boughs. Either way, the tradition of keeping Christmas decorations evergreen is carried on from year to year.

Gold silk roses and foliage in an onyx urn (*right*) are dressed for Christmas with the addition of fresh red carnations. The dried material is based in dry foam, so the living flowers must be put into water tubes prepared with wire 'legs' in the same way as for candles. Remember to fill with water each day. Many florists sell tubes, but if you cannot find any, impale a piece of soaked foam on top of the dry foam instead.

Permanent Flowers

Dried flowers and foliage – and many of the very beautiful
fabric flowers now available – can be great fun to arrange.
These arrangements are useful alternatives when fresh flowers
are not available from the garden, and a wonderful stand-by
for people who live in cities where fresh flowers can be
expensive in off-season periods.
Colourful arrangements made from last summer's flowers
and foliage can bring a note of nostalgia to long winter months
– just as the Victorians did when they kept dried flowers
between the pages of a favourite book to be reminded of a
special summer's day.
Included in this chapter are methods for preserving and
drying flowers, and how to make fabric flower designs for
display, head-dresses and posies.

In the winter months, when there are few fresh flowers to work with, dried flowers can provide particularly welcome decoration for the home. Large designs can fill empty fireplaces or the unused corners of rooms, and smaller arrangements can be made as centrepieces for occasional tables or mantlepieces. It is well worth putting time and trouble into your designs, since they will continue to look appealing for many months after you complete them.

With dried material, you can be very inventive in choosing containers since there is no problem of water seepage to consider. Pieces of driftwood, weathered wood and bark found on rambles might be employed, perhaps, or, for something more unusual, you could buy lengths of metal piping.

Dried flowers can also be used to decorate small boxes or wastepaper baskets, and they can make delightful pictures to hang on the wall. Miniatures can be really charming, but here it is important to choose material in the right proportion, and you will need tweezers to set the material in place. This may seem slow exercise but it can be very satisfying to complete such a picture. Old frames, which can be cleaned and resprayed, are often to be found in salerooms. Instructions for making a large picture are given below.

There is always a vast and exciting choice of dried materials available from the florists, but if you grow your own flowers many of them can be dried very easily at home.

Some subjects dry more attractively than others. For example, if delphiniums are cut just before maturity, they will

The montbretia stems, moss and achillea head (*above*) are enhanced by this unusual handmade container.

Find a suitable base for the picture. Then assemble the bouquet. Secure the outline at the tying point, before gluing it to the base. Once the outline is in place, add the filling piece by piece.

eventually dry out keeping an almost perfect colour. They are best cut when about half the spikes show full colour. They should then be stood in about 2 in (5 cm) of water and allowed to condition thoroughly. Then hang them upside-down in a dry, draught-free place until they gradually dry out. A light coating with clear spray will help to keep the florets in place.

Achillea retains its golden colour for several years.

Helichrysums and statice are very popular as dried materials. They supply a wonderful variety of both colour and form. For people who grow their own helichrysums, remember to insert a wire through the flower head as soon as it is cut as, once it dries, it becomes almost too hard to pierce. Try to insert the wire up through a short stem so that it does not show. Then hang the flowers upside-down in small bunches ready for using in your winter arrangements.

Hydrangeas also keep their colour, particularly the green and red varieties, but the pale blue variety turns brown, although it is useful for masking the foam. It is best to strip the foliage from hydrangeas before leaving them to dry out.

Molucella bleaches to a delicate cream tint as it gradually dries. Arranged with grasses or fabric flowers, it makes very elegant line material and is long lasting.

Roses, also, can be dried on their natural stems, while almost any flower head can be quickly and successfully dried in silica gel. You need quite a large quantity, for the heads should be arranged in layers and copiously covered with the gel. This is available from most good chemist shops or from specialist suppliers of flower arranging materials.

This hollow log (*right*) is an ideal container for dried material. The base is covered to protect polished surfaces.

Some people dislike the very thought of using imitation or permanent flowers and, certainly, there can be no substitute for the real thing, which is constantly changing, seasonal, exciting and sometimes unpredictable. Yet these flowers and plants that are made to imitate nature so exactly have a place in today's life-styles. They demand no conditioning, they will stay in place as they have been arranged and they will not wilt from lack of water.

Daffodils, daisies, ferns, gladioli, poppies and roses are all meticulously reproduced in a variety of sizes, colour, shapes and textures. In fact, there are very few flowers that are not now reproduced. There are also flowering plants, such as petunias, geraniums, hydrangeas and agapanthus, wisteria and laburnum, plus many other plants, which are correct in every detail and so convincing in appearance that one almost feels the need to water them.

Permanent flowers should be arranged with as much care as one gives to living material and the foam should be properly masked with either moss or foliage. In my view, bows of ribbon inserted into the centre of an arrangement do not make a substitute for careful masking. By all means add one or two bows if they enhance the general appearance of the arrangement. Be prepared to remove any unsightly stems and replace them with wire and tape. Some flowers, antirrhinums for example, are heavy and their stems will not support the flower head at the maximum stem-length. These have to be supplemented with extra wire or with slender canes attached with adhesive tape. This, of course, does not look very pretty, and should be used only if it can be hidden amongst the other flowers and foliage. The real thing has, of course,

1 To make a fabric flower arrangement, collect fabric flowers and foliage together in groups before preparing a container. Bright, mixed-coloured flowers have been chosen for this display.

2 First cut the correct size of brown floral foam and wedge it into the neck of a container and mask it with green moss.

3 Arrange the moss carefully so that moss and fabric foliage will appear very natural together.

4 Set the vertical and main lateral lines in position. The lateral material is set well back in the foam block to leave the front free.

strong enough stems to support the flower heads.

When buying permanent flowers and foliage, try to buy the best possible quality. These will withstand wind and weather, and having near permanent colours, will not fade in bright sunlight. They can also be washed providing you use very cool, soapy water (a detergent powder used sparingly is best). Rinse them carefully and lay them on a flat surface to dry naturally, then they will look as good as new.

5 Insert the remaining material in groups of similar colours to make the fullest use of a few flowers of each kind (*below*).

Asymmetrical arrangement (*left*) in mixed flame colours.
Below: Cream anemones and café-au-lait coloured foliage arranged on a cork base.
Right: A spring design of daffodils, freesias and polyanthus in a dove-grey compote.

Some fabric flowers are so realistic it is almost impossible to tell them apart from fresh material. Many of the actual flowers are really lovely, but sometimes the stems, calyx and foliage are not quite in keeping, so it is necessary to strip the flower from the stem and re-wire and tape it. You may think it is far quicker to work with fabric material since it requires no conditioning, and it is more or less indestructible. In fact, some permanent flowers need a surprising amount of preparation. However, the time spent is not wasted because your arrangement will last for just as long as you want it to.

Some fabric flowers are purely decorative and do not faithfully resemble any living material; they are useful simply from the point of view of colour, shape and size. Then there are those that are blatantly imitation but that are still very decorative and fun to use. For example,

huge gold and silver open roses, which, if used in the right place at the right time, are really effective. They can be used for gold or silver anniversaries, at Christmas or birthday parties or to decorate a special gift-wrapped parcel.

Fabric flower and foliage arrangements should be based in Oasis-sec or a similar product; ordinary foam used dry is not nearly firm enough and may easily break apart. Drihard is another product

that gives an extremely firm base, but being a type of cement it dries not only very hard but very fast. Thus one needs to work with both speed and precision since there is rarely a chance to change your mind once a stem has been placed.

Both foam base and Drihard should be masked, either with grey reindeer moss or ordinary green moss, both of which should be soaked in clean water to make them supple. The moss can then be

pinned to the base with small wire hairpins; it quickly dries, retaining its original colour.

Choose whichever moss blends better with the flowers; for example, spring flowers, daffodils, freesias and polyanthus would look more realistic based with green moss, while most dried material and the pale browns and creams of some fabric flowers look better with the reindeer moss.

Fabric flowers can be used to make a bouquet or for the head-dresses of a bride and her bridesmaids. The bride's mother might also trim her wedding hat with a design of silk flowers, perhaps, or make a handsome corsage for her outfit. On a more casual level, a single fabric poppy can cheer the most battered straw boater. The possibilities are seemingly endless.

Fabric flowers and foliage, while easier to handle than real flowers, need almost as much preparation as living material. Each flower has to be wired and taped, and the finished result should be at least as delicate as a real flower design. Carefully worked, however, a fabric flower design might last you a lifetime.

This charming bride's head-dress (*below*) is made in soft pinks to match the bouquet opposite. The flowers are wired and taped individually, and the finished arrangement is held on with hair grips (bobby pins) hidden underneath the foliage.

1 To make a fabric bouquet, the flowers and leaves are first wired and taped separately. The material is then arranged and secured at a central point and bound very tightly with fine wire. Final adjustments can be made to the positions of the flowers and leaves.

2 From the back, all lines should be seen to radiate from one central point.
3 The finished fabric bouquet (*right*). The handle has been bound with ribbon to make it more comfortable to hold.

Pressed Flowercraft

Introduction

HE marvellous thing about the craft of flower-pressing is that anyone can try it. Beginners and children can achieve pleasing results from the start and yet such is the scope of the craft that it also offers the expert the opportunity to produce truly exquisite work.

When I finally gave up the idea of returning to teaching to concentrate on my work with flowers, I was worried that my interest and pleasure in what had been a hobby might not last. How unjustified my worries were: I am still as fascinated by my work as I ever was.

Flower pressing is rewarding for many reasons, one of them being its potential for variety and change. Each flower is unique and therefore each design you make is unique. Your technique and style will develop with experience and you will probably look back on previous work and think, 'Well, it wasn't bad, but I like what I'm doing now better.' Suppliers are also selling an increasingly wide range of settings for the presentation of flower work. A few years ago presentation was limited largely to the creation of pictures, but there is now an enormous range of possibilities for producing small items like pendants, pill-boxes and a variety of beautifully-crafted trinket boxes. Settings can be used in so many different ways. (For example, individual gifts can be personalized by incorporating calligraphy into a flower design.) You should certainly not find yourself troubled by any lack of ideas!

The pleasure of working with flowers is central to every stage of the craft. I am occasionally asked where one can buy ready-pressed flowers, but I try to discourage people from doing this, because the collecting stage is such a vital and enjoyable part of the whole. What could be more delightful than to go out on a warm summer's afternoon to gather a collection of richly-coloured flowers and foliage for the press? When I return from such an expedition and tip out the precious contents of my basket in a tumble of colour on to my work-table, I know that collecting is an integral part of the process that I should hate to miss.

The flowers are then carefully consigned to the press. A really interesting stage comes six weeks or so later – the inspection of the now dried and flattened specimens. It is always a joy to see how much of their original beauty they have retained, and to observe which flowers press 'true', and which have undergone subtle colour changes in the process.

The most exciting stage of all is the creation of the designs, in the knowledge that even if you are not the world's most talented artist, the flowers are so beautiful to begin with that you should be able to produce lovely results. If you pick the right flowers in the right conditions and press them correctly; if you choose your colour combinations carefully; and above all, if you are receptive to the ideas suggested by the flowers, attractive designs will almost make themselves.

The next pleasurable task is that of matching the flowers and designs to the recipient. Why not make a wedding present using tiny wild pansies known as heartsease – in combination with 'lucky' heather? Or you could send pressed blooms collected locally to a home-sick friend far away. You can be confident that a floral birthday card will not be thrown away with the rest after a week or two, because, in a world in which so much is mass-produced and expendable, a design that has been carefully hand-made with real flowers is something to keep and value.

Although I entirely respect the conservationists' view that rare flowers should *never* be picked, I cannot agree with those who object to the picking of any flowers at all. Nature is bountiful, and provided that we pick sensibly, the countryside should not suffer for our having been there. But what a difference pressed flowers from summers long past can make to our homes where designs will live on bright and beautiful.

I began by saying that flower-pressing is a craft that anyone can try, and I hope that I shall convince you that this is true. The first three chapters contain all the essential information about equipment, materials, pressing techniques, and some of the flowers and foliage most suitable for your work. Chapter 4 gives practical suggestions on how to make attractive designs and Chapter 5 contains details on how the wide variety of settings now available can be put to good use in presenting your work. There is no substitute for practice, though, or for the personal touch. If you love flowers and enjoy making beautiful things you will find that your efforts will be repaid in good measure with all the satisfaction and joy that the craft has to offer.

127

Equipment and Materials

NE of the great advantages of this craft is that you can start without spending very much money. In fact it may well be that you already have most of what you need at home, and that a variety of everyday household objects will now become the essential tools of your craft. It is a good idea to assemble the following items in one place. (Try to keep them there too!)

PRESSING EQUIPMENT

The most important piece of equipment is, of course, something in which to press the flowers. This could be simply a large book, or it might be a flower press specifically designed for the job.

An out-of-date telephone directory is ideal as a pressing book because it has the right sort of absorbent paper. Books with glossy pages are unsuitable as they can encourage mildew. A second advantage of a phone-book is that it does not matter if its spine is eventually damaged by the thickness of the layers of flowers. (Naturally it would be unwise to use the family bible or any other treasured volume for this purpose!) Whatever large, expendable book is used, additional weight is necessary for successful pressing. Such weight could be provided in the form of other heavy books or bricks.

Although the phone-book method can be perfectly effective, I prefer to use a press. This is because it puts the flowers under greater pressure and therefore speeds the drying process. Also, carefully prepared flowers are rather less likely to be disturbed by having the separate layers of blotting paper and corrugated card placed on them from above, than by the sideways action of closing a book.

Many craft shops and quality toy shops now sell flower presses. These are fine – but avoid making the mistake of buying the smallest ones, which measure about 4in (10cm) square. The disadvantage of these is that, although they are pretty and can be used effectively for small flowers, they have severe limitations if you want to press such essential elements as grasses and long, gracefully curving stems. The ideal size for a press is, in my opinion, about 9 in (23 cm) square. Larger ones can become very heavy and, unless they have some

RIGHT *A selection of satins in colours suitable for use as design backgrounds.*

129

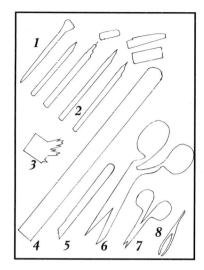

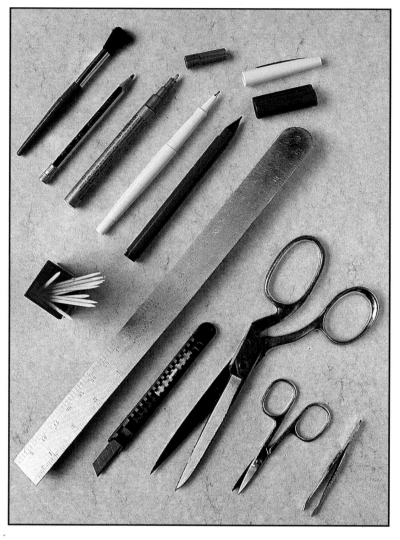

ABOVE AND RIGHT *Useful tools*
1 A fine soft brush to tease off slightly sticky pressed specimens from their blotting paper beds, to move delicate flowers around during design work, or to brush surplus pollen from flowers such as buttercups. 2 Pencils and pens for a variety of jobs, from indexing storage books to doing decorative line work. 3 Cocktail sticks or toothpicks, for applying tiny amounts of glue to flowers. 4 A ruler – metal if possible – to ensure straight edges. 5 A retractable craft knife for cutting card and mountboard, preferably of the type that has a blade with several snap-off sections, so that the blade is always sharp. 6 Scissors: a large pair for cutting paper, fabric and other materials and 7 a smaller pair for use with plant material. 8 A small pair of tweezers for picking up delicate plant material or for working with various jewellery-type settings available for presenting flower designs.

ABOVE *A typical pressing book, used here for pressing heather. Additional weight is provided in the form of two bricks.*

special device for maintaining pressure in the middle, the two pieces of wood which sandwich the pressed material may develop a tendency to bow or warp. The result of this is that the flowers in the middle are under less pressure than those around the edge, and are therefore at risk of shrivelling or becoming mildewed.

MAKING YOUR OWN PRESS

This is relatively simple and should ensure that you get exactly what you want in size, weight, the number of layers, and so on.

If you are intending to take this craft seriously, you may find it worthwhile to make two or even three presses at the same time, because in the summer months there is often such an abundance of material for pressing that is hard to manage with only one.

MATERIALS FOR MAKING A PRESS **1** Two pieces of sturdy wood such as plywood, measuring about 9 in (23 cm) square and ½ in (1 cm) thick (9-ply is ideal and should not warp). **2** Four 3in (8cm) bolts with wingnuts to fit.

ABOVE *A press in the making.*

3 Three large sheets of blotting paper. **4** Some stiff corrugated card which can be cut from packing material such as boxes from supermarkets.

ABOVE *A finished press, together with a lightweight travelling press.*

Rub down the surfaces and edges of the plywood with sandpaper. Place the two pieces together, one on top of the other, and drill holes large enough to take your bolts in each of the four corners, about ¾in (2cm) from the edge; fix the bolts into the bottom piece of wood, gluing the heads securely into position. Cut 12 8in (20cm) squares of blotting paper, trimming off triangular pieces at the corners to accommodate the bolts; cut 7 pieces of corrugated card of the same size and shape. Starting and ending with card, interleave two pieces of blotting paper with each layer of card. Place this card and blotting paper 'sandwich' on the wooden base; locate the top piece of wood on the bolts and secure the wingnuts.

You might also find it useful to make a lightweight travelling press, an ideal companion on a country expedition. It can be made on the same principle as the sturdy press, but for convenience it should be smaller –

ABOVE *An interesting gradation of colour is seen on this velvet-backed picture. Note the relatively light colour around the edge where the fabric is most firmly gripped by the locking plate and the darker tone in the middle of the picture. The flowers are anaphalis (pearly everlasting).*

perhaps 6 in (15 cm) × 8 in (20 cm) – and lighter. Substitute thick hardboard for the plywood, and two sturdy tight-fitting elastic bands for the nuts and bolts.

STORAGE EQUIPMENT

You will need to find some means of storing pressed material in good condition until you are ready to use it. This should be easy because, whether or not you have used old telephone directories for pressing, they certainly make excellent means of storage. You may find it useful to keep several of these books, each one reserved for a different type of plant material.

Some people prefer to store each type of flower in an individual bag. This method is fine, if the bags are porous so that the flowers can 'breathe'. Plastic bags are not recommended: they could trap any remaining moisture. The ideal bag for the purpose is one which has a paper back for porosity, and a cellophane front for visibility. If bags are to be used, a convenient means must be found of keeping them under some pressure. Inside telephone books perhaps?

ABOVE *A range of attractively coloured writing papers which can be used as design backgrounds.*

MATERIALS FOR DESIGN WORK

When you are ready to begin making designs, you will need a range of materials. Most of these should be as easily available as the equipment described previously. Items required include design backgrounds, such as paper, card or fabric, as well as glues, and some protective coverings.

Paper or card should be of good quality and have an attractive colour and texture. In addition to the materials that can be purchased from art and craft shops, the range of ordinary coloured writing papers now available offers a delightful choice; moreover, plain areas of thin card are often to be found in suitable colours and sizes on attractive packaging material.

My preference is to use fabric as a background for most flower designs. This is because its range and subtlety of colour and texture is even greater than that now available in paper and card. Patterned and heavily textured fabrics are obviously not suitable for design backgrounds, but almost any fabric that looks good with flowers will do. The ones I like best are velvet and satin.

ABOVE *Some of the many richly coloured velvets which make ideal backgrounds for flower designs.*

ABOVE *Two examples of the sort of colourful fabric swatches which you might be lucky enough to acquire from the furnishing fabric departments of large stores.*

ABOVE *Design backgrounds backed with a self-adhesive covering to give them more body. (Apply this backing before cutting the background to size.)*

Velvet has a rich depth of colour which changes according to the angle at which you look at the design, and becomes lighter in colour where greater pressure is applied (around the edge of a picture, for example, where the veneer pins or locking plate grip most firmly). Satins have a beautiful sheen, and are suitable for use with the most delicate flowers.

Acquiring fabrics should not involve too much expense. It is not necessary, for example, to purchase the most costly dress satins: lining satins can be just as attractive and, although velvet is usually expensive, you require only small pieces and might discover just what you need on the remnant counter. Remember also that either furnishing or dressmaking fabric will serve the purpose; any plain-coloured leftovers from other handiwork can be put to good use. Best of all, you might be fortunate enough to acquire one or two out-of-date swatches of plain fabric colour samples, as used in large furnishing fabric departments. You would than have an amazing range of colours from which to choose.

All but the sturdiest fabrics are easier to work with if they are given more body by being backed with a self-

adhesive covering (of the sort normally used for such purposes as covering shelves). Any pattern is unimportant, for it will not show.

The most important type of glue required is the one that sticks the flowers to their background. For this purpose, I prefer to use a latex adhesive which can be applied in tiny amounts on the end of a cocktail stick. You may also need other types of glue from time to time, including one for bonding paper and card. This is most conveniently available in the form of a solid adhesive stick.

Once a design has been glued into position, it should be covered in some way that ensures permanent protection for the flowers. A variety of materials may be used for this purpose: clear self-adhesive covering film, varnish, resin, acetate or glass. All these materials and the many specialized settings in which your designs may be presented are discussed in Chapter 5.

ABOVE *The various materials which may be used to protect finished flower designs.* **1** *Clear varnish* **2** *Acetate* **3** *Coating resin* **4** *Glass* **5** *Clear self-adhesive covering film*

Techniques

 SUGGESTED earlier that you can suc-
ceed in this craft, even without any
highly developed artistic ability,
because the flowers themselves create
much of the beauty of the finished
effect. This being so, it is obviously
vital that the quality of the pressed
specimens in your designs is as close as possible to the
perfection of the growing flowers. Accordingly, this
chapter gives a step-by-step guide to techniques, from
collecting the flowers to mounting them in their settings.
Its aim at each step is to give hints on how to retain their
original brightness and beauty.

FLOWER COLLECTING

If you are lucky enough to have somewhere to grow
your own flowers, your work may begin long before the
collecting stage. There is the delight of choosing the
seed packets most likely to produce blooms good for
pressing. Then there are the pleasures of planting the
seeds, tending the young plants and watching them
grow to maturity. For the purposes of this chapter, I
need only start from the point at which you are ready to
pick the flowers.

When collecting flowers for pressing, the aim
should always be to pick the best specimens in the best
conditions. This is relatively easy with flowers picked
very near your home since you can choose just when to
pick them. Several factors should be taken into account
when deciding on the optimum time for picking.

Flowers must be picked at the right stage in their
development. This stage is usually reached shortly after
they have emerged from the bud, when their colour is at
its richest. Occasionally, buds are more useful to the
flower-presser than the open form, as in the case of
tightly closed dark-orange montbretia buds. Many
designs are enhanced by the use of both buds and open
specimens of the same flower, so it is often a good idea
to press them in both forms. But do not succumb to the
temptation of trying to enjoy the beauty of the flowers
on the plant for as long as possible, picking them for
pressing only just before they fade or drop. This does
not give good results.

RIGHT *A collection of specimens
just removed from the press on
their blotting paper sheets.*

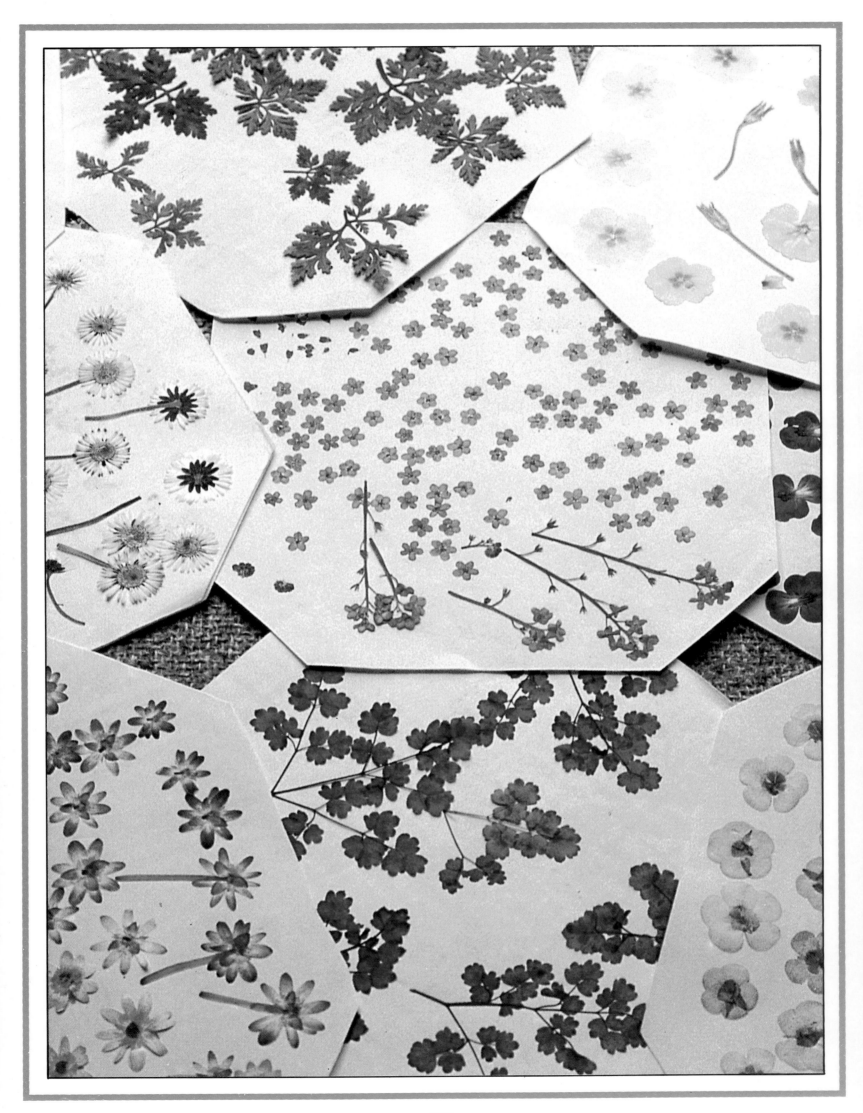

ABOVE *Collecting celandines for pressing.*

ABOVE *Collecting forget-me-nots for pressing.*

Foliage also has to be picked at the right stage of development. The very young leaves of eccremocarpus, for example, and those of *Clematis montana* emerge from the press a striking black colour. If picked when too mature, they turn out a much less inspiring flat green. Even grasses should be watched for the right stage – their delicate spikelets should be open, but not so far developed that they are ready to shed their seeds all over your designs.

Pick each species early in its season when the plants are lush and sappy – they will press far more successfully than those which appear later in the season.

Another important factor to consider is the weather. Damp is the flower-presser's main enemy: it encourages mildew. Specimens should therefore be collected on a dry day when any droplets of water from the showers of previous days are likely to have evaporated.

The time of day is also important: a sunny afternoon is the best time of all. Even a fine morning may be damp with dew and, by early evening, some flowers will have closed for the night.

The final luxury of picking flowers locally is that it is practical to pick a few specimens at a time and to put them straight into the press before there is any possibility that their condition can deteriorate.

When travelling farther afield to collect flowers, it may be more difficult to ensure ideal conditions. However, the guidelines listed above still apply. The major problem is likely to be keeping the flowers fresh. If they have wilted by the time you arrive back home, it will be much more difficult to press them successfully. I can suggest two methods of maintaining freshness.

One is to use a travelling press, as described on page 11, and press the flowers as soon as possible after picking them, preferably in a sheltered spot. When you arrive home, the card and blotting paper 'sandwiches',

ABOVE *A collection of flowers sealed in an inflated plastic bag in order to maintain their freshness, as it was not possible to press them immediately.*

with the flowers undisturbed inside, can be simply transferred to the main press. (Alternatively, if the travelling press is not likely to be required again for a while, you can put it under an additional weight and leave it exactly as it is.)

The second method of maintaining freshness is to carry around several airtight plastic bags. Collect the specimens directly into the bags – not too many in each or they may crush each other. When you have finished collecting, blow air into each bag, as if you were blowing up a balloon, and secure the top with a flexible tie. This air cushion serves to prevent the flowers from becoming crushed, over-heated or dried out. They should then arrive home – even many hours later – as fresh as when they were picked.

Remember to pick only perfect specimens. Pressing cannot improve a substandard bloom – and your designs can only be as beautiful as the individual flowers that make them up.

ABOVE *A perfect buttercup specimen.*

PREPARATION FOR PRESSING

The flowers and foliage collected will be of many different types, shapes and sizes. It may not always be possible

1

2

3

4

TOP *It is a simple matter to prepare buttercups for the press. Give them a good start by squeezing the centre of the open flower between thumb and finger, taking care to spread the petals evenly. Then place them, face downwards, on a layer of blotting paper or a page of your pressing book.*

ABOVE *Pressed specimens of flowers that need some preparation before successful pressing can take place.* 1 *Love-in-a-mist and* 2 *London pride should both have their projecting seedboxes removed. The seed box behind the dog rose* 3 *also needs removing. The multi-flowered heads of elderflowers* 4 *must be separated into small sprays while hydrangea florets* 5 *must be pressed individually.*

to put them straight into a press without some form of preparation. Various techniques are involved.

The simplest flowers to press are those that are flat or like a shallow dish in shape. Buttercups are a good example of this type and can be persuaded easily into a new two-dimensional state.

Remove any part of a flower which might impair the appearance of the whole after it has been pressed. When flowers are to be pressed in the open form, for example, it is wise to remove stems from all but the sturdiest, in order to prevent them from bruising or deforming the petals under which they lie. For the same reason, certain parts of flowers – like the green calyx which sheathes the back of a primrose are best removed.

Another reason for removing flower parts is to facilitate the transformation into the two-dimensional. Both love-in-a-mist (devil-in-the-bush) and London pride press well, once the seedboxes which project in front have been removed. The same can be said of the single dog rose after the careful removal of the seedbox from behind the flower.

TOP *It is a good idea to remove both the stem and the calyx of a primrose before pressing. The calyx might otherwise bruise the delicate petal under which it lies.*

ABOVE *Forget-me-not stems should be prepared for pressing by removing some of the individual flowers to prevent overcrowding. The spiral of buds at the top of the stem may also be pressed separately.*

Multiple flowers may be prepared in a variety of ways. Some, like elderflowers, can be pressed effectively either as a whole or in small sprays, as long as the groups of florets are spread out as much as possible when being placed in the press. The flower-packed heads of a hydrangea, usually bearing well over 100 florets, may seem a daunting prospect until it is realized that each one can be removed and pressed separately, like any flat flower. One of the multiple flowers which best repays preparatory work is the forget-me-not. If the stems are pressed unprepared, the many flowers – which had plenty of space in their three-dimensional growing state – will be overcrowded and develop unattractive marks wherever they have overlapped the stem or each other.

ABOVE *The three-dimensional daffodil can be sliced in two and pressed in profile.*

If you thin them out, however, you will be doubly rewarded with graceful curving stems of undamaged flowers, and by the individual 'thinnings' which press into tiny circles of sky-blue perfection.

So far, I have considered only flowers that can be converted relatively easily to the two-dimensional. But what of truly three-dimensional flowers like daffodils, roses and carnations? It could be argued that these are best left alone by the flower-presser.

Daffodils can be pressed effectively by removing the seedbox and slicing through the trumpet, after which it is possible to press the two resulting 'profiles'. The same slicing technique can be used on very small rosebuds; larger ones, however must be treated differently: remove the green sepals for separate pressing, and then carefully peel the delicate satin-smooth petals from the bud so that each one can be pressed individually. (When making rose designs later on, you can reconstruct 'buds' by using petals and sepals, or fully open 'roses' by building up layers of invididual petals and using the centres of rock roses as false, but fairly true-to-life, middles.)

ABOVE *All but the smallest rosebuds must be separated into individual petals before pressing. Press the green sepals for the later reconstruction of rosebuds.*

ABOVE *This detail from a wedding bouquet picture shows rose petals reconstructed into open roses and carnation petals in both open flower and bud form.*

Carnations can be treated by the same 'separate petal' procedure. Their pressed petals make realistic 'buds' when used in combination with sections of the green sheath-like calyx (see the wedding bouquet illustrations).

It is always sensible to place only flowers of the same thickness in any one layer of the press. This eliminates the risk of putting the flatter ones under insufficient pressure, which could cause shrivelling or encourage mildew. But what if a single flower is itself of uneven thickness? This can sometimes be a problem. One occasionally sees daisies for example whose petals have become spiky because they have not been as heavily pressed as the middles. In the case of such small flowers this problem can usually be overcome by giving the yellow middles an extra firm squeeze before pressing. The solution is not so simple with the bigger daisies, or with other large daisy-type flowers you may want to press. These flowers have middles which are so significantly bulkier than their surrounding petals that it would be impossible to apply even pressure to the whole flower without the use of a 'collar'. This is a series of newspaper

TOP *A single daisy-type chrysanthemum being pressed by the 'collar' method.*

ABOVE *Clumps of moss should be allowed to dry out in a warm room for several hours before being separated into small pieces for pressing.*

RIGHT *Position the layers of blotting paper and card in the press taking care not to disturb the flowers being covered.*

or blotting paper circles with the centres cut out to accommodate the thick middle; the correct number of layers of paper can be placed underneath the petals to even up the thickness.

As you gain experience you will develop all sorts of personal techniques for preparing particular flowers and other types of plant material. You may, for example, find it helpful to use a rolling pin to 'pre-press' a particularly thick stem of, say, *Clematis montana*. Alternatively, you may decide to slice it in two before pressing. You will also discover exceptions to the 'rules' – particularly, perhaps, to the one which decrees that all plant material should be placed in the press as quickly as possible. Moss, for instance, almost invariably comes from a damp habitat and is therefore best left in a warm room for a few hours before pressing. It may also be a good idea to allow stems to wilt a little, so that they become more amenable to being pressed as curves.

One final general point about preparation: although you are not necessarily considering the finer details of design at this stage, it is nevertheless helpful to keep the likely eventual designs in mind when you are arranging material in the press. Once the specimens are dried, they are more or less fixed in shape. Any 'persuasion', such as encouraging snowdrop heads to hang at a natural angle, should therefore be done now.

PRESSING

The aim of this stage is to dry and flatten the flowers in such a way as to ensure that they come out of the press as bright and as beautiful as when they went in. There are various hazards from which they must now be protected. The three major ones are undue disturbance, mildew and incorrect pressure.

UNDUE DISTURBANCE

Once they have been prepared for pressing, flowers should not be disturbed any more than is absolutely necessary. This means that when the press is being filled, its layers of card and blotting paper must be carefully placed one on top of the other, so that the flowers do not move from the position in which you have set them, and none of the leaves or petals is

RIGHT *When using a pressing book, avoid disturbing or damaging specimens by gently rolling closed the pages.*

RIGHT *Good, mildew-free specimens of carnation and rose petals and calyces.*

accidentally folded over. Similar precautions should be taken when closing a pressing book: its pages should be gently rolled closed over the precious contents. You should, particularly in the early days, resist the temptation to 'see how they are getting on'. Partly pressed material is very limp and, once misshapen, is difficult to reshape correctly.

MILDEW

Mildew is the most serious risk at the pressing stage. It can be heartbreaking to open the press after several weeks and find everything inside covered with a damp grey mould. This should not happen if the necessary precautions are taken.

Make sure that flowers are under sufficient pressure. Pressing-books must be adequately weighted, and the wingnuts of presses must be checked every day or two during the first week. This is because as the material in a press dries out, it becomes less bulky so that the nuts need tightening to maintain the pressure.

Keep your presses in a dry, airy place.

To avoid the spread of any mildew if it does occur, make sure that there is plenty of space between the flowers on each layer, and that the layers themselves are well separated by corrugated card or several intervening pages.

Do not add any new, moisture-laden material to a press or book already containing drying flowers.

In spite of my advice not to disturb the flowers unnecessarily, it is nevertheless sensible to inspect a few of them after a week or so to check for damp or mildew. If any is found, a more thorough check is indicated, during which you should throw away any even slightly mildewed specimens, and change damp blotting paper

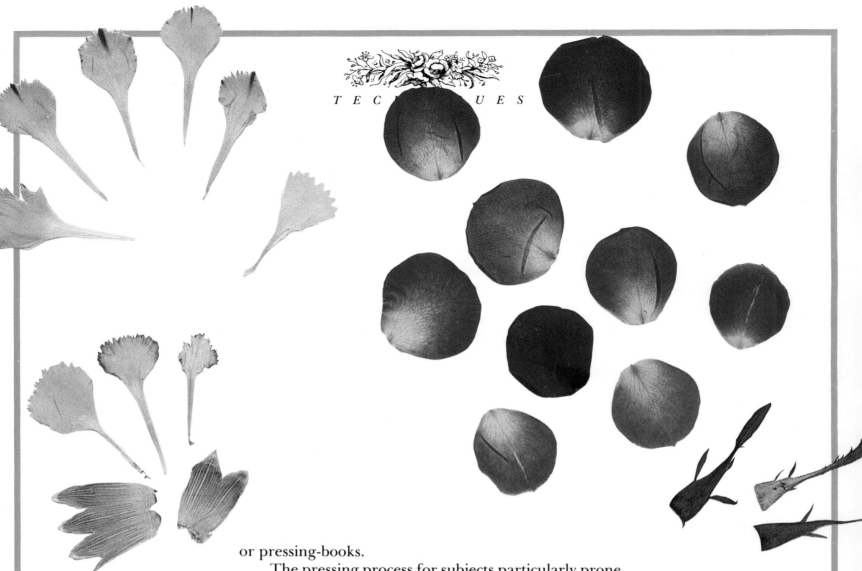

or pressing-books.

The pressing process for subjects particularly prone to mildew, such as roses and carnations, may be best *started* in any particularly warm dry place or airing-cupboard. But I would not recommend this for all flowers, or for any flowers for more than a few days. They can become dry and brittle if left too long.

INCORRECT PRESSURE

Just as too little pressure can put flowers at risk, so over-pressing can also present a problem. It usually occurs only when a press containing layers of corrugated card is used. Such card is normally invaluable because its corrugations aid ventilation and help to prevent the spread of damp. Also its flexible thickness does much to maintain an even pressure on bulky subjects. If precautions are not taken, however, it can cause imperfections on delicate petals. Primroses, for example, pressed between single sheets of blotting paper sandwiched between this card, could emerge from the press with corrugations imprinted on their petals. You may feel happier using the book method for these tender specimens, but you can still use the press if you insert additional layers of blotting paper, or if perhaps you replace the card altogether with several thicknesses of newspaper.

A final note on pressing: it is worth mentioning that both blotting paper and pressing-books can be re-used indefinitely, as long as they are perfectly dry and free from mildew.

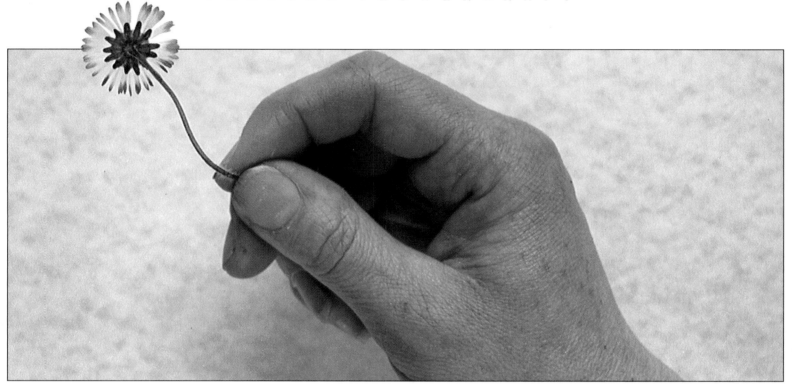

PRESSING DURATION

Traditionally, the pressing process takes about six weeks – a slightly shorter time for small, dry specimens, and a little longer for those that are larger or more moisture-laden. A simple test of whether a flower is ready for use is to select a specimen still on its stem, and hold it up by the base of the stem. If it stands upright, it is ready; if it flops, it should be returned to the press for a little while longer.

At the height of summer, when flowers are at their most abundant, you may find you need a press for new material before its original contents have been in for long enough. It is reasonable, in such circumstances, to transfer the flowers carefully to well-weighted storage books at any time after the first ten days. If you do this, remember to label them clearly with the pressing date and not to use them in designs until the full six-week period is complete.

Other ways of shortening the time in the press involve the use of modern appliances. The aim of pressing flowers is to dry and flatten them so you might be forgiven for thinking that you could do this most efficiently with a domestic iron! In fact, if plant material is ever needed urgently (or an otherwise good flower has a creased petal), it is possible, with the iron on a low-heat setting, to press sturdy flowers or leaves between sheets of blotting paper. This process should be followed by a few days under pressure in a warm dry place. And after the iron, what next? The microwave, perhaps? I have no direct experience of this, as yet, but have heard of its use in speeding the drying process.

LEFT *A pressed daisy standing upright. It is now completely dry and ready for use.*

RIGHT *A collection of specimens just removed from the press on their blotting paper sheets.*

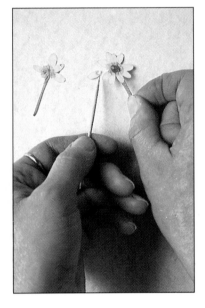

ABOVE *A celandine with a missing petal being repaired with a good petal from another blemished specimen.*

REMOVING FLOWERS FROM THE PRESS

Now comes the pleasure of looking through the wealth of lovely pressed material from which you will soon be creating designs. If all has gone well, you will have many perfect two-dimensional representations of the original specimens in a variety of rich colours. Larkspur duplicate the shades of the growing flowers; the little annual phlox (Pride of Texas), undergo subtle colour changes; the young leaves of eccremocarpus show an even more dramatic change.

Of course, it would be over-optimistic to believe that everything you press will turn out perfectly and it is sensible to discard any specimens that come out of the press badly discoloured or faded, damaged or distorted. There will always be a small proportion of these, which would spoil your designs if used. (Do not, however, be too quick to throw away flowers that are only slightly damaged, for it may be possible to amalgamate two blemished blooms into one perfect specimen.)

It is worth mentioning here that although most flowers obligingly slide straight off their pressing backgrounds into their new storage accommodation, others need a little gentle persuasion before they will move. The tiny individual forget-me-nots, for example, have a tendency to stick to blotting paper, and each one needs to be patiently teased off with the soft tip of a fine brush. Fingernails or even tweezers may cause damage.

STORAGE

Once flowers have been pressed, they must remain permanently under some form of pressure, whether in storage or in their final settings. Only in this way will they remain in good condition; any exposure to air will put them at risk of reabsorbing moisture.

ABOVE *Some specimens, like the individual flowers of forget-me-nots, have a tendency to stick to blotting paper. They can be teased off with a small soft brush.*

RIGHT *Pressed specimens may be stored in books or cellophane-fronted bags. It is a good idea to arrange them in a logical order and to index or label books so that flowers are not disturbed any more than is necessary.*

All my pressed specimens are stored in a series of old telephone directories. These are excellent for the purpose because they are freely available, heavy enough to keep the flowers in good shape, and large enough not to overcrowd the specimens. Also, their absorbent pages deal with any possible traces of remaining moisture. Another possibility is to store each type of flower in individual cellophane-fronted, paper-backed bags as described on page 12. Storage books and bags should, like presses, be kept in a dry airy place and, if piled one on top of another, should be occasionally rearranged so that they are evenly ventilated.

Each type of flower should have its own bag or section of book, and all the pressed material should be arranged in a logical and easy-to-find order. This is because the 'do-not-disturb-unnecessarily' rule remains as relevant as ever, and repeated searches through randomly-stored flowers for a particular specimen greatly increase the risk of damage.

I keep separate books for miniature flowers, larger flowers, leaves, grasses, and so forth, and within each book the specimens are arranged in the order in which

they appear during the year. As a consequence of this, I know that early flowers, are usually to be found somewhere among the Collinses, while the midsummer blooms live with the Joneses, and the autumn species with the Wilsons! This information is a little too vague, however, so at the beginning of each book I keep a list of page numbers detailing exactly which flowers appear where. As an alternative to such a list, labels identifying flowers can be attached to the relevant pages or bags. These precautions should ensure that you can always find a particular flower quickly and easily, and with the minimum of disturbance to the rest.

Great care is needed when removing specimens from bags and when replacing them if they are surplus to requirements. Also, when turning the pages of storage books you should try to make sure that the contents do not slip towards the spine. If everything collects in this area, the book becomes misshapen – and so do the flowers.

DESIGN BACKGROUND

Before you can begin designing, you need to choose your background. Whatever this is to be made of, it must be prepared in such a way as to ensure that when the flowers are fixed to it and it is mounted in its setting, it will remain smooth and unwrinkled. Card is the simplest background to use, needing little preparation other than cutting to size with a craft knife. Paper, on the other hand, may need sticking to a sturdier back-

LEFT *The choice of background colour is important especially when dealing with flowers that are not the most marvellous colour-keepers. These celandines are being mounted on a dark green satin against which they will still look beautiful even if they fade a little.*

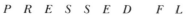

ground to keep it flat. Fabric must also be backed in some way, its preparation depending on the type of fabric and on the nature of the setting in which it is to be used. (For a consideration of how to prepare fabrics for particular settings, see Chapter 5.)

Choosing background colour is largely an artistic decision, but it has one technical aspect. Most pressed flowers lose some colour over the years and some fade relatively quickly. It is therefore inadvisable to use very pale backgrounds unless there is a good reason to be confident about the colour fastness of the flowers being used. When – as in the case of celandines – you know that they will lose much of their brilliance during the first year, choose a strong background colour.

WORKING AREA

It is not until the point at which you actually begin making your designs, that the nature of your working space becomes critical. For all the tasks previously described, such as pressing flowers and putting them into storage books, almost any fairly large space will do. (My preference – particularly when transferring to storage – is to use the floor, where I am often to be found surrounded by a wide area of brightly coloured pressed flowers on numerous sheets of blotting paper.)

Before beginning design work, however, it is essential to prepare a suitable working surface. It should be in a room that is dry and, as far as possible, dust- and draught-free: the slightest breeze could be enough to ruin a design on which you have spent many hours. It is therefore a good idea to have available a sheet of glass with which to cover your work if you have to leave it, even for a few minutes, before it is stuck down. (And it goes without saying that sneezing in this area is not recommended!)

The working space should be large enough to accommodate your storage books, design background, tools, glue and everything else. If at all possible, it should be an area that is not going to be required for any other purpose in the immediate future. A design, or series of designs, may take several days to complete, and you will become very frustrated if you decide to work on the dining table and have to remove everything each time you have a meal!

HANDLING FLOWERS

You will be able to remove the sturdiest flowers from their storage books, and move them around on the design background, simply by using your fingers. When dealing with more delicate specimens, however, it may

ABOVE *The best way of handling a delicate specimen is to apply gentle pressure to it with a slightly moist finger tip. The flower* *should then 'stick' to your finger for long enough to enable you to move it into the desired position.*

be helpful to use small tweezers to pick them up, and the tip of a fine brush to move them around on the design.

The method I prefer for the most delicate flowers of all is to moisten the tip of my forefinger very slightly, by touching it just inside my lip. I apply gentle pressure to the flower to be picked up, which then usually sticks to my finger sufficiently well to allow me to transfer it to its new position. The great advantage of this technique is that I do not risk damaging my most fragile specimens by trying to get either fingers or tweezers underneath their petals.

STICKING DOWN FLOWERS

Once a design is in its setting, the glass – or whatever is used to protect your work – should be holding it so firmly in place, that nothing could possibly move. It is, however, so difficult to get an 'unstuck' design into its

ABOVE *When sticking down a design, use a cocktail stick to apply a tiny spot of latex adhesive to the base of the thickest part of each flower.*

ABOVE *Sticking down overlapping flowers.*

setting without any of its components moving out of position, that it is almost essential to glue down every single piece.

This does not mean that the whole area of each flower has to be firmly stuck to its background. The smallest possible amount of adhesive should be applied, on the end of a cocktail stick, to the back of the thickest part of each flower or leaf. Stems should have tiny spots of glue dotted along their length; fine materials like grasses and tendrils need stroking in only one or two places with a lightly glued stick.

You will soon find out if you are using too much glue, because it will show through delicate petals. Worse still, it may squeeze out from underneath and mark the background. If this happens with a latex adhesive, it is often possible to 'roll off' of the offending glue by rubbing the marked area with a clean finger.

When you become experienced and are sure of the effect you are trying to create, you may choose to stick down each part of the design as you go along. If you are less experienced, or experimenting with new ideas, it is probably better to lay out the whole design before you stick any of it. Then, taking care not to disturb the surrounding flowers and leaves more than necessary, you can pick up each one separately and gently glue it into position. Where flowers overlap, you must, of course, stick down the underneath ones first.

COLOUR RETENTION

Colour is not everything. The beauty of a pressed-flower design resides in far more than this, and wonderful effects can be achieved by using the subtlest and most muted of colours. The fact remains, however, that it is lovely to see flower pictures that capture the original brightness of nature. So I am not surprised that the question I am most frequently asked by the people who look at my work is, 'How do you keep the colours so bright?' I have no single piece of 'magic' to offer in reply, just the advice that if you press the right flowers (see Chapter 3) and use the techniques outlined in this chapter, you have every chance of success.

Your responsibility for helping to retain colours does not end at the point where the flowers are safely in their settings. The position in which they are then displayed is important. No pressed flower design should be constantly exposed to direct sunlight (so do not stand paperweights on sunny windowsills). Remember also that moisture can continue to be a problem so a room like a damp conservatory could be a disastrous place to hang a flower picture.

There is, of course, one means by which it is possible to make certain that flowers retain their colour. This is the technique, recommended by several books on the subject, of colouring flowers permanently with poster paints. Decide for yourself on this matter. It is not a technique I use, because to my eyes, the hard,

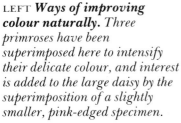

LEFT **Ways of improving colour naturally.** *Three primroses have been superimposed here to intensify their delicate colour, and interest is added to the large daisy by the superimposition of a slightly smaller, pink-edged specimen.*

BELOW LEFT *It is possible to achieve beautiful effects without using bright colours. This box lid has a design of creamy elderflowers and cow parsley, and dark herb Robert foliage backed on a beige velvet.*

1 2 3

4 5 6

ABOVE *Colour testers and the lessons to be learnt from them.*
1 Forget-me-nots, spiraea (both white and pink), saxifrage and the veined petals of the ballerina geranium all keep colour well. The alpine phlox and the purple lobelia (as opposed to the blue one) do not. 2 Montbretia buds and hypericum keep colour beautifully. 3 All the flowers in this frame (blue lobelia, heuchera, lady's mantle, astrantia and the heather florets) have proved reliable. 4 This

artificial colours of paint fail to blend with the subtler natural shades of flowers. If I feel that a flower is going to lose colour to the point at which it will no longer be attractive, I would prefer not to use it at all.

Although I am not prepared to 'cheat' by using paint, I am entirely in favour of 'cheating naturally'.

When dealing with the fine translucent petals of such flowers as the primrose, I am happy to put one, or even two, additional flowers on top of the original one to intensify its colour. A daisy with a bright yellow middle but thin petals can be superimposed on one with a discoloured middle but beautiful pink-edged petals. Similar 'tricks' can be employed with foliage. Except when making 'botanical pictures', I often substitute leaves which are more attractive or keep colour better than a particular flower's own leaves. When working with snowdrops, for example, I usually use the similar but (to me) much prettier white-lined crocus spikes.

The whole subject of colour retention in pressed flowers is fascinating, and the only way to study it satisfactorily is to observe the various changes which take

*frame shows that the larkspur and delphinium (**right**) are better colour-keepers than the love-in-a-mist (**left**). 5 The hardy fuchsia is seen to keep colour reliably. 6 The 'everlasting' helipterum and anaphalis included here are still bright as is the darker of the rock roses.*

It is apparent from these colour testers that, while foliage which presses black or silver maintains its original colour, almost all green foliage fades.

LEFT *Snowdrops arranged with the attractive, white-lined spikes of a crocus plant.*

ABOVE *Cowslips whose yellow flowers have turned green.*

place over the years. This requires patience, of course, but you will, in time, be rewarded by knowing which flowers are going to retain their colours most reliably.

I now have a series of 'colour testers', comprising a wide variety of flowers mounted in frames so that I can see what the passing years do to them. The flowers and foliage fall into three categories: those that keep their colour well; those that pale down but are still beautiful enough to be worth using against the right background; and those that, regretfully, I have not pressed again. One of the greatest surprises with respect to a bizarre colour-change was the once limpid yellow cowslips: they are now bright green!

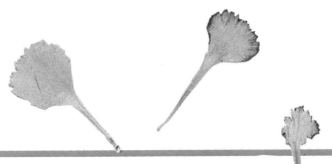

CHAPTER THREE

What to Press

 T IS customary when discussing this craft, to refer to flower-pressing, but of course that term is only a convenient general description of an activity to which there are many aspects. Although flowers will probably be the main elements in most of your designs (and for that reason a survey of flowers takes up by far the largest section of this chapter), the scope of your work will be enormously limited if you have collected only blooms. Foliage of all sorts is needed to give added dimension and interest, and extra possibilities are added by collecting a wide range of other plant material such as stems, tendrils, seeds, seedpods, ferns, grasses, mosses, and even seaweeds.

It would be marvellous if, once you had assembled the necessary equipment and materials, and knew how to set about picking and pressing the flowers, you could simply go outside and gather whatever you fancy. Sadly, however, this is not always practical because, although many flowers are ideal for pressing, others are just not worth bothering with. There are no hard-and-fast rules to predict for certain what will press and what will not, but there are some useful general guidelines. It is helpful to consider three characteristics of each candidate for pressing: its size, shape, and degree of succulence.

Unless you intend to make very large pictures, you should be looking for relatively small flowers, avoiding the largest of the cultivated blooms of which gardeners are so justly proud. (If a particular over-large flower is especially attractive to you, however, it may be useful to return to the plant a little later in its season, by which time it may have thrown off side-shoots that produce manageably smaller flowers.)

Sometimes the beauty of a flower resides largely in its shape, and although it is usually possible to separate the individual petals and reconstruct them in two-dimensional form after pressing, this is not always worth while. The beautifully spurred aquilegia (columbine) for example – so descriptively called 'doves round a dish' – is best left alone by flower-pressers who can work more successfully with its flatter-faced relative, the larkspur.

None of the really fleshy flowers – like orchids or the larger lilies – press successfully. Nor do those tender plants whose high moisture content makes them a prey to the early frosts. (Begonias and the exotic fuchsias fall into this category.) A good test for succulence is to squeeze a flower firmly between finger and thumb. If moisture or – worse still – colour comes out, it is a fair indication that this is a flower to be avoided, for the end result of pressing is likely to be a squashy brown mess on the blotting paper. Conversely, if when squeezing the flower your fingers remain dry, there is reason to proceed with a greater degree of optimism. The sort of flowers that can be collected most confidently of all are those that can be successfully air-dried. Thus flowers such as larkspur, astrantia and hydrangea, and any of the everlasting varieties that are flat enough, all press and keep colour beautifully.

Once you have a general idea of the sort of flowers to look for, you may proceed with some confidence to experiment with those that are available. The following pages list those that I have found particularly useful. Choosing from these lists may allow you to get off to a good start and help you to avoid some disappointments in the early days. but remember that they are only a starting point. There are many more flowers with pressing potential than those referred to below, and there is no substitute, in terms of interest or reliability, for your own experiments. You will occasionally be disappointed when a small, dry, flattish flower, which seemed like an ideal subject for the press, loses all its colour in a short time. But you will, on the other hand, be pleasantly surprised when another less likely subject turns out to be perfect. (My greatest discovery of this sort was the snowdrop. For years I avoided it, thinking it unsuitable because of the cold, damp conditions in which it grows, and because I feared it might be a little too moisture-laden to keep its beautiful pure white. But what a reward when I finally tried it! It has become an indispensable part of my flower collection.)

RIGHT *It is fascinating to observe how one area of nature mimics another. These delicately veined skeleton holly leaves resemble the structure of insect wings.*

INSET *A skeleton seed pod of the Cape Gooseberry. These are truly 'magic lanterns' for within their beautifully veined and still closed lanterns, they hold imprisoned the spherical papery remains of the fruit, with the seeds still inside.*

PLANTS AROUND THE WORLD

The fruits and vegetables that we are now able to buy are increasingly international and the same is true of the flowers in florists and nurseries. Cultivated flowers are invariably descended from wild flowers or are actually wild flowers from another part of the world. For example many cultivated lobelias, montbretias and heathers grown in northern temperate countries originated in South Africa; fuchsias have similarly been exported from New Zealand, and the lovely *Helipterum roseum* and several other everlasting flowers from Australia; the flowering currant, heuchera, the *Limnanthes*, larkspur, phlox, hydrangea and golden rod are from the United States.

The experimentation that I commend to all flower-pressers is very important. If you are unfamiliar with some of the flowers listed below, identify similar members of the same plant family that grow near you and try pressing them instead. Violets and pansies (Violaceae), vetches (Leguminosae), heathers (Ericaceae) and daisies (Compositae) are all members of families that have a worldwide distribution. (The Composites that I have included in this section should be pressed using the collar method if they are to be used whole.)

In North America, there are many different species of viola. Perhaps the most immediately attractive is the fern-leaved violet, *Viola vittata*, which is rather like *Viola tricolor*. You might also try some of the large number of North American pea plants (Leguminosae) and any heathers that grow in your area. The most obvious Composite to try is *Gaillardia pulchella,* otherwise known as Indian blanket, or, more descriptively, firewheels. Both the swamp rose and the prairie rose should press satisfactorily.

Members of all four family groups mentioned above abound in southern Africa. There are many lovely heathers, of which the pink bridal heath, *Erica bauera* and the similarly-shaped green form of *Erica filipendula* seem the most attractive. The selection of available Composites is stunning; the many species of *Arctotis, Dimorphotheca* and *Felicia* are only a few of the possibilities. You could usefully experiment with any of these with a fair degree of optimism as to the results.

In New Zealand and Australia, there is again considerable potential in the vetch and viola families. In the absence of native heathers, try instead the pink *Epacis impressa* and the smaller-flowered white *E. microphylla.* Any everlasting flower flat enough to press is also a candidate for attention, so it would be well worth trying small specimens of the strawflower or yellow paper daisy, *Helichrysum bracteatum;* the soft grey-green flannel flower *Actinotus helianthi* might also be worth a try.

The stately buttercups of New Zealand are somewhat fleshier than the European ones, but any flower from this family (Ranunculaceae) should at least be the subject of an experiment, as should the smaller varieties of native fuchsia.

Wherever you are, there are flowers that will press. The challenge is to go out and find them. It should not be difficult if you remember the general recommendations given above – that is, if you choose flowers with the right characteristics and are prepared to experiment.

CULTIVATED FLOWERS

Gardens are a rich source of flowers for pressing – but please do not miss out this section if you are not lucky enough to have a garden of your own. Some of the flowers listed below can be grown fairly easily in tubs, window boxes or even indoors in pots on a windowsill. Alternatively, generous friends may invite you to look for pressing material in their gardens. Failing this, it is always a good idea to keep an eye on the florists' shops and market stalls (pushcarts). Once, when my larkspur crop failed, I was able to press enough of these indispensable flowers to satisfy a whole year's needs from one enormous and inexpensive bunch purchased locally.

I have arranged the following list of garden flowers roughly in the order of their appearance (in most areas of the world) from early spring to high summer. I think this arrangement may perhaps be a little more helpful than the more usual alphabetical one because, as the seasons progress, you will have an idea of what you might look out for next.

SNOWDROP (*Galanthus nivalis*)

Use only the 'single-skirted' varieties and press in bud or profile. Do not try to press them open because this looks unnatural. Consider using them with the spiky white-lined leaves of the crocus.

DAFFODIL (*Narcissus minimus*)

In spite of their three-dimensional shape, ordinary daffodils can be pressed by the method described on page 21. It is probably simpler, however, to stick to those varieties of the extensive *Narcissus* family which can be pressed whole. These include the miniature daffodil, named above, which is small enough to be pressed in profile, and the lovely narcissus, 'Soleil d'or', which has several golden flowers on each stem. The trumpet sections of these flowers are relatively flat and will, if you make a few small snips in them, lie against the outer petals so that you can press them open.

HEATHER (*Erica carnea*)

The various winter-flowering heathers provide wonderful splashes of colour at a time when this is otherwise in short supply. The pink varieties are particularly attractive. The flower spikes can be pressed whole, but what comes out of the press tends to be too solid looking to use as it is. So discard the woody stems and spiky leaves, which usually drop off anyway, and use only the tiny bright pink flowers.

ANEMONE (*Anemone blanda*)

A delicate daisy-like flower with blue or mauve petals surrounding a yellow middle. Choose only those with the deepest colour.

PRIMULA (*Primula* spp)

There are many different species of this valuable flower, some of which have a bloom on each stem, whereas others grow in clusters. Most of them are potential 'pressers' and it is well worth while experimenting. The yellow and orange flowers usually press true, while the reds and purples darken. It is advisable to remove the green calyx and to trim off that part of the back of the flower which would otherwise lie behind one of the delicate petals and mark it.

SPIRAEA (*Spiraea arguta*)

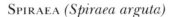

A shrub that produces large numbers of tiny white flowers on slender arching stems. Each flower should be snipped off and pressed separately. A little later on in the season look out for *S. bumalda,* which produces clusters of crimson flowers.

ALYSSUM (*Alyssum saxatile*)

This is the sweet-smelling yellow alyssum which is often grown together with aubrietia. It is not a marvellous colour-keeper, but is too pretty to pass over completely. Press its minute round buds and tiny, just open, flowers.

FLOWERING CURRANT (*Ribes sanguineum*)

Another spring-flowering shrub, valuable for its small bell-shaped flowers which hang in clusters. Press buds and flowers separately.

FORGET-ME-NOT (*Myosotis alpestris*)

Invaluable, and well worth the trouble of snipping off some of the flowers for separate pressing. This creates uncrowded stems which also press well. The spiral of buds at the top of each stem is particularly attractive.

London Pride (*Saxifraga urbicum*)

This produces sprays of small pink flowers on each stem. Flowers should be pressed separately after the removal of the projecting sticky seedboxes. This is a painstaking process, but you will be rewarded with little pink circles, spotted with deep red, which look delightful in miniature designs together with forget-me-nots. Try also the larger-flowered saxifrages which grow one to a stem. The rosy-coloured ones press beautifully, producing pink, almost translucent petals.

Poached egg plant (*Limnanthes douglasii*)

A quickly spreading hardy annual, producing dish-shaped flowers which are easy to press and very attractive. Putting one or more directly on top of another intensifies their delicate colour.

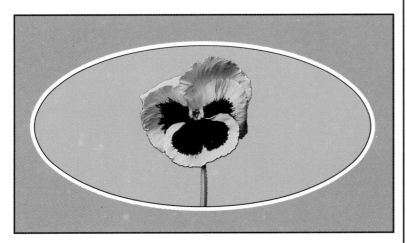

Pansy (*Viola tricolor hortensis*)

These are found in many different sizes and colours. (Yellow flowers keep their colour particularly well.) My preference is for the smaller ones and those with the most defined 'faces'.

Heuchera (*Heuchera sanguinea*)

One of the most useful small flowers, and one of the best red ones for keeping colour. The bell-shaped blooms grow many to a stem. Pick them when the lower flowers are fully out and the top ones still in bud, for then the stem is spread enough to be pressed whole.

Rock rose (*Helianthemum nummularium*)

This flowers profusely in the summer sunshine, in a wide variety of bright colours. The petals are fragile but, handled with care, should press perfectly. They are best gathered early in the day for, later on, the petals have a tendency to drop. Do not discard these 'bare' middles however, because they make realistic centres for reconstructed roses.

ROSE (*Rosa* spp.)

I have been surprised to read in more than one book on this craft that pressed roses 'always turn beige or brown'. This need not be so if the petals are pressed individually and are taken from mature buds rather than from open flowers. In the case of miniature roses, it is possible to avoid pressing the petals separately by slicing the buds in two, and pressing each half in profile. The smallest rose of all is the much loved *Rosa farreri persetosa*. This is a single variety, so the tiny buds can actually be pressed whole. They look delightful in simple designs which also use their miniature leaves.

DELPHINIUM (*Delphinium elatum*)

This is a tall perennial with colours varying from pale blue to deep mauve. It proudly contradicts the fallacy that blue flowers do not keep their colour. (I have seen pictures of pages taken from a scrapbook over 100 years old in which the delphiniums are still blue!) Each flower on the stem should be pressed individually, but may still be rather large for many designs. If this is the case, wait for smaller flowers on the side-shoots, or consider pressing the petals separately.

LADY'S MANTLE (*Alchemilla mollis*)

Tiny yellow-green star-shaped flowers grow on intricately branched heads. Press these in small sprays – but not too soon. Let the heads open out a little, or the pressed spray will look solid and lumpy.

LARKSPUR (*Delphinium consolida*)

More useful than its perennial relative, this annual has an even bigger range of colours which are bright, press 'true', and do not fade. Could you ask for more?

LOBELIA (*Lobelia erinus*)

Another 'true-blue' colour-keeper. Pick only a few at a time for its petals curl quickly.

GYPSOPHILA or BABIES' BREATH (*Gypsophila paniculata*)

These sprays of tiny white flowers are very useful as delicate 'space fillers' to soften the outline of designs.

LOVE-IN-A-MIST or DEVIL-IN-THE-BUSH (*Nigella damascena*)

Not such a reliable colour-keeper but so beautiful, with its blue flower-head surrounded by fine misty green foliage, that it is still a good choice if mounted on a strong background colour. Remove the seedbox before pressing.

ST JOHN'S WORT (*Hypericum elatum*)

This shrub species produces masses of small, yellow, dish-shaped flowers, measuring about 1 in (2.5 cm) across and having a lovely central boss of golden stamens. Remove the seedbox before pressing. The stamens are even more spectacular on the shorter but larger-flowered *H. calycinum*, known as the rose of Sharon or Aaron's beard.

PHLOX or PRIDE OF TEXAS (*Phlox drummondii*)

The short annual species of phlox, each stem of which bears many flowers in dense heads. Pick the florets singly and trim off the backs. The various colours undergo subtle changes during pressing.

GRANDMOTHER'S PINCUSHION (*Astrantia carniolica*)

The true flowers of this interesting plant are tiny, but the surrounding bracts look like the petals of a larger flower. These bracts may be white and green, pink, or a maroon-red. Their pointed shape gives them a geometric appearance, like the points of a compass.

CLARY (*Salvia horminum*)

This is another plant with insignificant flowers whose beauty is in its bracts. These are pink and purple and keep colour well. They can be used in designs as the 'petals' of imaginary flowers.

HYDRANGEA (*Hydrangea* spp.)

Many species of this plant are excellent for pressing. The pinks, blues, and even the underdeveloped greens press well once the florets have been separated from the densely-flowering heads.

PERUVIAN LILY (*Alstroemeria aurantiaca*)

This lovely perennial, which grows in a variety of colours, is a good example of a three-dimensional flower whose individual petals are so beautiful that it really is worth while pressing them separately, prior to reconstructing them into imaginary two-dimensional flowers. I have to admit to having seen them more frequently in florists' shops than in gardens – but perhaps this is something we should try to change, for they are not difficult to grow and the species named above is hardy.

MONTBRETIA (*Crocosmia x crocosmiiflora*)

Pick these graceful curving stems when most of the flowers are still in bud. They then retain their deep orange colour. Any of the trumpet-shaped flowers which are already out may be pressed separately, open or in profile.

GOLDEN ROD *(Solidago* spp.)

Remove the curved plumes of tiny golden flowers from the tall stems. These may then be used whole, or separated for miniature designs.

The last three flowers mentioned, anaphalis, sea lavender and helipterum, are all of the 'everlasting' type more usually seen in three-dimensional dried-flower arrangements. They are more or less dry when picked, and need only to be hung up for a week or two in a warm, airy place to complete the process. They then need pressing very briefly just to flatten them, and they can subsequently be relied upon to retain colour for years. The best everlasting specimens for pressing purposes are, of course, those which are not too bulky.

ANAPHALIS or PEARLY EVERLASTING *(Anaphalis yedoensis)*

Clusters of pearly white flowers grow on a single stem. When they are dry, remove the seed heads from the middle of each flower to reveal the beautifully detailed, green-centred faces. Press each flower separately.

FUCHSIA *(Fuchsia magellanica)*

The flowers of this bushy shrub are smaller and less moisture-laden than those of most of its exotic relatives. These are the qualities which make it the hardiest of the fuchsias and the best for pressing. Press the lovely pendant flowers in profile, leaving them on their curving stems and taking care to arrange the petals evenly. The scarlet stamens are so striking that you might occasionally choose to use them separated from the flower (for instance as butterfly antennae).

SEA LAVENDER or STATICE *(Limonium sinuatum)*

This grows in a variety of bright colours. Press each of the florets separately.

HELIPTERUM *(Helipterum roseum)*

A beautiful pink daisy-like flower with papery-dry petals.

WILD FLOWERS

Before beginning my list of wild flowers, I must emphasize one point. A number of rare species is now protected by law, and in some places it is forbidden to pick even the common ones. The following rules should therefore be observed.

Never pick rare flowers. Never pick even common flowers from places where they are scarce or protected. Remember that if you pick all this year's crop, there will be no seeds for next year. However abundant the flowers may be, never pick more than you need.

Fortunately, most of the best wild flowers for pressing are the very common ones. There are, however, one or two exceptions. It is now unusual, for example, to come across large numbers of primroses or heartsease (wild pansies) in the countryside. Luckily, this need not be a problem because, in response to the growing public awareness of the need for conservation, a number of the larger seed-packaging companies have brought out collections of wild flower seeds, which are now readily available. So, if you are keen to collect and conserve the less common wild flowers, consider reserving an area of your garden for them.

I have, once again, listed the flowers approximately in order of appearance (from spring to high summer). It is even more important with wild flowers to have some idea about when to expect them because, unlike their cultivated counterparts, many wild flowers may be too far away to present a daily visual reminder that now is the time to gather them, and some of them have a relatively short season. So it is as well to be forewarned, in order to avoid the frustration of a trip to the countryside during which you suddenly realize that you have missed the best of the celandines, for example, and will have to wait until next year to collect good specimens.

This list is shorter than that for the cultivated flowers, but this does not mean that wild flowers are any less valuable to the flower-presser. In fact, I think the reverse is true. I should not want to do without either, but if I had to make a choice, I would choose the wild flowers for their simple beauty – and for the more practical reason that, by their very nature, they are more likely to display the required characteristics of good pressing flowers; that is, to be small, two-dimensional and relatively dry.

DAISY *(Bellis perennis)*

This most indispensable of all wild flowers certainly lives up to its Latin name, for not only does it recur profusely year after year, it also has a long season, in many areas appearing before most flowers we would particularly associate with spring, and continuing to bloom well into the autumn. Moreover, it is an ideal candidate for pressing. The best specimens are those with pink-edged petals (probably the result of cross-pollination with the cultivated varieties).

COLTSFOOT *(Tussilago farfara)*

This is the only one of the dandelion-type flowers to press satisfactorily because, unlike the others, it has a flat middle. It is therefore easy to spread the surrounding spiky 'petals' evenly. Again, it is worth considering using its equally attractive underside.

CELANDINE *(Ranunculus ficaria)*

These brilliant yellow starry flowers open their glossy petals to reflect the spring sunshine. They will pale down after a year or so to a lemony-cream colour, but they are so beautiful in form that, if mounted against a dark background, they will still be attractive.

COW PARSLEY *(Anthriscus sylvestris)*

This is just one of the many useful species of the Umbellifer family. Others to look out for are fool's parsley, earthnut, burnet saxifrage, rough chervil and wild carrot. All have branched umbels, each topped with 'rays' or clusters of tiny flowers. To make a representation of such intricate structures in paint, embroidery or lace would indeed be work for a patient artist. But nature makes it easy for the flower-presser, by offering us this family of plants, the different members of which adorn the countryside throughout the late spring and summer. Press whole umbels or separate rays.

PRIMROSE *(Primula vulgaris)*

A delicate yellow symbol of springtime. Always remove the green calyx before pressing and use two or more superimposed flowers to intensify the colour of the translucent petals.

ELDERFLOWER *(Sambucus nigra)*

These frothy cream flower-heads have many florets to a stem. Heads may be pressed complete or in sprays. Used individually or in clusters in a design, the creamy-beige flowers add delicacy to your work.

HEARTSEASE OR WILD PANSY (*Viola tricolor*)

This small wild pansy has perhaps the most appealing 'face' of any flower. I so much prefer it to its larger cultivated relatives, that I encourage it to grow in my garden. I take care, however, that I plant it in a relatively inhospitable position because plants growing in thin soil produce tiny dark flowers, small enough for the daintiest designs.

SPEARWORT (*Ranunculus flammula*)

A very useful small relative of the buttercup, though not as easy to find. Look for it in damp places.

BUTTERCUP (*Ranunculus acris*)

Beautiful and easy to press, buttercups grow abundantly in many areas. Avoid roadside flowers if possible, for they are usually dusty. *R. repens* is the equally attractive creeping buttercup.

BIRD'S FOOT TREFOIL (*Lotus corniculatus*)

An attractive meadow flower, best pressed in bud because the open flower becomes three-dimensional, and because the deep yellow buds are richer in colour and sometimes, if you are lucky, tipped with red. This is a member of the vetch family, or Leguminosae, many of whose members, yellow or purple, are well worth considering for pressing.

DOG ROSE *(Rosa canina)*

This charmingly simple wild rose is unlike its lusher, fuller-petalled garden relatives in that it can be pressed whole. Remove the seedbox from behind the flower.

HEATHER *(Calluna vulgaris)*

I prefer this common wild variety to its stiffer cultivated counterparts. It grows on moorland and you can almost see the wind in the graceful curves of its stems. Its foliage, too, is attractive and does not drop.

LEAVES

It is possible to make effective designs using leaves only, but though flower pictures without foliage may be pretty, they are bound to look unnatural – for where can flowers ever be seen growing in the absence of greenery?

It follows, therefore, that it is necessary to press a good selection of leaves. As with flowers, there are some which press better than others and some general guidelines may be given regarding which these are. Types of leaves to avoid are the fleshy ones, like those of African violet; needles, like those of pine or many of the cultivated heathers; and thick evergreens, such as laurel, which refuse to dry out properly. Most other types of leaves press successfully, and the choice depends on finding specimens that are manageably small, interesting in shape and attractive in colour. A few of the most valuable are listed below, starting with those of wild plants, working through to cultivated ones, and progressing – by way of the fruit and vegetable gardens – to creepers, and finally to trees.

HERB ROBERT *(Geranium robertianum)*

The small purple flowers of this plant are fairly ordinary, but the beautifully-shaped, slightly hairy leaves are invaluable. They are often made even more attractive in the later part of the year by a tinge of red.

EARTHNUT *(Conopodium majus)*

Many members of the Umbellifer family have delicate leaves which press well. This is the most dainty, especially when gathered in the spring, before the white flowers appear. Press as soon as possible after picking, or the leafy sprays tend to wilt and close up.

COMMON MEADOW RUE *(Thalictrum flavum)*

The tiny yellow flowers are insignificant but the leaves are beautifully angular. Press both the bright green leaves of midsummer and those which turn yellow as the plant approaches the end of its season.

SILVERWEED *(Potentilla anserina)*

This is another indispensable plant, whose feather-edged leaves are grey-green on top and silver underneath. They can be used whole in large designs and are equally beautiful when segmented into smaller pieces. Silver-leaved plants are generally useful for the attractive variation they bring to designs and because they do not change colour. The following two cultivated plants also offer particularly beautiful silver leaves.

CINERARIA (*Cineraria maritima*)

The 'Silver dust' variety has delicate fern-like leaves.

PYRETHRUM (*Chrysanthemum/Pyrethrum ptarmica folium*)

Also known as silver feather, this plant has intricately-shaped leaves which can be used whole or separated into small sections for use in miniature designs.

RASPBERRY (*Rubus idaeus*)

Even fruit bushes deserve attention, particularly for the silver underside of these leaves.

CARROT (*Daucus carota*)

Not to be outdone, these vegetables also produce delightful leaves. Their delicacy is not so surprising when you realize that they belong to the Umbellifer family.

CLEMATIS (*Clematis montana*)

The young leaves turn a striking black when pressed.

ECCREMOCARPUS or CHILEAN GLORY FLOWER (*Eccremocarpus scaber*)

A useful annual climber, whose tubular orange flowers are best left alone but whose interestingly-shaped leaves also turn black on pressing.

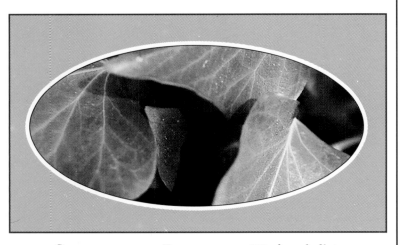

COMMON IVY or ENGLISH IVY (*Hedera helix*)

Press the smaller leaves of the dark green varieties which keep colour better than the variegated ones.

VIRGINIA CREEPER (*Parthenocissus quinquefolia*)

These beautifully shaped leaves are at their best in their glorious autumn colours.

TREE LEAVES

It is possible to press the leaves of many trees successfully. Experiment and think about pressing, both in the spring, when the leaves are small, tender and sappy, and in the autumn when they achieve their most glorious colours. (By this stage they are so dry that they need to be pressed only briefly.)

MAPLE (*Acer* spp.)

All the members of the large acer family of trees and shrubs are grown for their ornamental foliage, and produce a variety of beautiful shapes and colours.

BEECH (*Fagus sylvatica*)

Both the green and copper varieties are best pressed in spring. The young leaves of the copper beech give an autumn feel to designs.

OAK or ENGLISH OAK (*Quercus pedunculata*)

Press the immature leaves in spring time.

SUMACH (*Rhus* spp.)

Best picked in autumn, when the leaves turn brilliant orange or scarlet. Look for smaller leaves on the creeping suckers.

FLOWERING CHERRY (*Prunus* spp.)

There are many varieties of these lovely trees. The leaves of most of them are beautiful in autumn and best collected just before they drop. Their lovely colours, shape, and feathery outline make these leaves perfect for Christmas card 'robins'.

OTHER PLANT MATERIAL

Flowers and leaves are by no means the only suitable subjects for pressing. Other types of plant material are suggested below. The plant names listed under each heading are only a few of the many possibilities.

STEMS

These are usually best pressed separately to avoid marking the flower petals. Press a collection of stems, ranging from the slender, graceful ones – like those of primroses and daisies (which can be substituted for the stiffer stalks of flowers like celandines) – to the larger swinging curves of such climbing plants as clematis.

TENDRILS

An extra dimension may be added to a design by the use of tendrils, which can improve it in a quite unintended way. Use the springy coils from the sweet pea (*Lathyrus odoratus*), other vetches, and eccremocarpus.

SEEDS

The loveliest are probably the feathery whirls produced by many of the different varieties of clematis. (I use these not only in flower designs but to form the tails of my cherry-leaf birds.) The winged seeds of the sycamore maple *(Acer pseudoplatanus)* can also be used to make similar simple representations of moths' wings. Some 'natural artists' work only in this medium (see illustrations on pages 64–6) using attractive seeds, such as those of zinnia, marigold, cosmos daisy, lettuce, grass, reed, caraway and sesame.

SEED-PODS

There are several of these which can be attractively used in two-dimensional designs. Honesty *(Lunaria annua)* produces shiny silver discs when the stems have been dried and the dark outer pods removed. Herb Robert, being a member of the cranesbill family, produces a seed-pod illustrating that name. Even the seedbox of the common poppy *(Papaver rhoeas)*, though three-dimensional as a whole, can create a beautiful little 'wooden flower' if its fluted top is carefully sliced off.

FERNS

These grow throughout the world and many of them press satisfactorily. Three that I use regularly are the delicate maidenhair fern *(Adiantum capillus-veneris)* with its lovely sprays of green, and two bigger ferns: the common bracken or brake *(Pteridium aquilinum)* and the prettier hay-scented buckler fern *(Dryopteris aemula)*. Pick young fronds, but consider splitting them into more manageable sizes before pressing. Consider adding variety to designs by the occasional use of the underside of the leaves with their attractive, dark, spore-producing circles.

GRASSES

Most grasses press well because they are fairly dry to start with. For this reason they may conveniently be pressed directly in the books in which they are eventually to be stored.

The delicate grasses are perhaps the most useful because they help to achieve a lovely soft outline when used for filling the spaces around a design. But try to press a variety of specimens: green and brown; straight and curved; solid and feathery.

Some grasses you might consider collecting include: the delicate bents *(Agrostis* spp.) and meadow-grasses *(Poa* spp.) in their many varieties; the aptly named quaking grasses *(Briza* spp.), most useful for flower designs in their smallest form *(B. minor)*; the different types of brome *(Bromus* spp.), all of which may be pressed whole and then have their variously shiny or downy spikelets removed for separate use in designs. These spikelets – especially the hairy ones – make realistic 'bodies' for leaf or petal butterflies, as do the individual whiskers of wild oats *(Avena fatua)*.

MOSSES

Mosses are especially useful in miniature designs, where small, curving pieces can create the effect that a combination of curved stems and leaves might have made in a larger design. It is not until one begins collecting for the press that one realizes how many different shapes, sizes and shades of moss there are. My favourite ones are the bright green *Eurynchium praelongum*, found commonly on shaded tree-trunks; the darker *Plagiomnium undulatum*, with its intricate tracery of wrought-iron-like shapes, and the sturdier *Mnium hornum*. Because mosses usually grow in very damp places, I prefer to allow them to dry out in a warm room for a few hours before separating them into small pieces for pressing.

SEAWEEDS

Seaweeds are now often put at the bottom of a list of suggested subjects for pressing. This would not have been so in the 19th century when they were widely collected for use in design work. Gather the prettier, more delicate types of seaweed; rinse them thoroughly to clear them of sand; drain and blot them well and lay them on blotting paper. You can then arrange their fine filaments into attractive shapes with a soft brush. It is advisable to use several sheets of blotting paper and to change the outer layers frequently until the seaweed is completely dry. There is no need to emulate the 19th-century method of sticking the seaweed to its background, which was to use the skin of boiled milk!

NCE you have a collection of good pressed material, you are ready to proceed with confidence to the design stage. Sadly however, this is just the point at which many people come to a standstill. 'I have books full of pressed flowers, but I've never done anything with them because I just don't know where to begin.' This is a *cri de coeur* heard all too frequently (and I can remember I felt like that too), but now I want to say in reply, 'Don't stop now, when you are only a step away from the most rewarding phase of the craft. Have confidence. You will certainly be able to make attractive designs if you let the flowers help you.'

The design section of books on flower-pressing, with their references to 'contour', 'balance', 'harmony' and other technicalities can be somewhat daunting to a beginner. I would therefore like to suggest an absolutely practical approach. Of course, this is not the only way to begin, but it will, I hope, build up confidence as you progress. Try working through the following steps, using your own choice of flowers, introducing variations whenever you wish, and abandoning my suggestions altogether at the point at which you find your own style.

START SMALL, START SIMPLE

Choose a small setting and be prepared, at this stage, to rely entirely on the beauty of one individual flower to create the design. Choose your flower with care, for you will not get away with such complete simplicity unless it is a perfect specimen, and unless it is sufficiently intricate or visually interesting to satisfy the eye. Background colour and texture are all-important, and I would recommend the use of fabric for the additional interest it can provide. (Try placing your flower on a variety of different backgrounds to decide which one enhances it most.) Finally, try to ensure that your work is technically perfect, for a badly positioned flower, a roughly cut-out piece of fabric, or a single spot of unwanted glue can mar simple designs.

An ideal flower for this purpose is the astrantia. With its tiny flowers and surrounding pointed bracts, it needs no further embellishment. To add depth to the beautiful pink-tinged specimen used in this paperweight, I

RIGHT **Start small, start simple.** *Four 'designs' each relying on the beauty of the individual flowers to create the finished effect.* **1** *Love-in-a-mist* **2** *Burnet Saxifrage* **3** *Astrantia* **4** *Wild Carrot.*

1

2

3

4

have placed it on top of a second, slightly larger, plain green and white flower, and have chosen a pink background to bring out the colour of the central flower.

Another particularly suitable candidate for the simple approach is love-in-a-mist (devil-in-a-bush), with its dark green central stamens and fine misty-green foliage that surrounds the flower. A little judicious re-arrangement might be necessary if this foliage is not evenly spread, but basically it is still the simple beauty of the flower which does the design work.

The lacy flower-heads of the Umbellifers are also sufficiently intricate to 'stand alone'. The two species I particularly favour are the wild carrot, used back-to-front to show the beautiful arch-shaped foliage which lies under the flowers, and the burnet saxifrage, with its spoke-like stems. One additional flower-head makes a centre for this design.

You should as you gain experience succeed in making larger and more elaborate pressed flower pictures. But for sheer simple beauty, you may never make anything to surpass these small, one-flower 'designs', in which the patience, care and technique are yours but the art is all nature's.

ADD A LITTLE EMBELLISHMENT

Begin again with a single central flower, but this time, use a slightly larger setting and add some pieces of foliage, radiating from the centre. Then introduce some other tiny flowers in colours that blend both with the central specimen and with the background.

In the simplest of the three designs shown, two primroses have been placed one on top of the other to intensify their pale colour. The shape of the petals has been allowed to suggest the position of the five pieces of herb Robert leaf, and three single florets of golden rod, whose deeper colour blends with the pale primroses, have been arranged in each of the spaces thus created.

The *Limnanthes* design on the darker green also uses two superimposed central flowers, this time with the pale green leaves of a delicate fern in the shape of a six-pointed star, and the heads of cow parsley, making a dainty space-filler.

The design using the central larkspur is the most complex, using two contrasting types of foliage, with the pink heather florets as space-fillers. (When I first placed

FAR LEFT ABOVE ***Add a little embellishment.*** *Foliage and extra small flowers have been added to the main central flower in each of these three designs.* **1** *Primrose with golden rod and herb Robert foliage.* **2** *Larkspur with heather and both silver and green foliage.* **3** *Limnanthes with cow parsley and fern.*

LEFT ABOVE ***Make a symmetrical design.*** *Use a selection of regularly shaped flowers and rely on symmetry to produce an attractive effect. The two larger designs are based on anaphalis, the round one has the underside of a regularly shaped astrantia for its centrepiece and the oval centre is earthnut. The pendant design is made of forget-me-nots and elderflowers.*

this design on its background, I used only four pieces of each type of foliage, but the effect was so square-looking that I added another piece of each.)

ABOVE ***Use nature as designer.*** *These simple designs show snowdrops and heather just as they grow naturally.*

MAKE A SYMMETRICAL DESIGN

Having made some semi-regular designs based on a single central flower, you will want to progress to more complex work. One way to introduce this is to try something completely symmetrical. Pressed-flower pictures should always be balanced and in proportion, but they certainly need not be symmetrical. Indeed, it would be very limiting to make only regular designs. These can, however, be beautiful, and my reason for considering them here is that it is not difficult, even for a beginner, to think out a symmetrical design that works well. This does not mean that they are easy to make from a technical point of view. They demand quite as much care and patience as any other design, and a far greater degree of precision in choosing and positioning flowers and foliage, which must be carefully selected for their regularity of both size and shape.

Try working with the beautifully regular anaphalis (pearly everlasting), together with the leaves of herb Robert. If these are unobtainable, you may be able to find enough regular specimens of the equally attractive common daisy. Among the smaller flowers that work well in symmetrical designs are forget-me-nots, London pride, spiraea and elderflower. You will see from my examples that this sort of design succeeds equally well in round or oval settings. It could also be easily adapted to fit a rectangular frame.

USE NATURE AS DESIGNER

You should by now be beginning to think about making 'free' designs. A lovely way of doing this – if you are still feeling unsure of yourself – is to use nature itself as designer. What could be more simply effective than an oval picture, backed on green velvet, depicting snowdrops as they appear in a spring garden, or the graceful curves of heather as it blows on moorlands?

This sort of design looks deceptively simple, but be prepared for it to take quite as long to make as something more intricate, because it is so important that it looks just right. Snowdrops should be the correct size in relation to each other, their heads hanging at natural angles; and the shapes of the heather stems should look as if they really are growing together. It may be necessary to look through most of your specimens of a particular flower before you find a perfectly natural-looking group, but the end result should make the time spent well worth while.

If you are a botanist at heart, you may well decide that this is the type of flower-work for you. You could then go on to make a variety of botanical pictures of individual species, using both open flowers and buds,

ABOVE *Each of these simple botanical cards uses the flowers, buds and leaves of one species (heartsease, daisies and celandines).*

RIGHT *This design of buttercups, golden rod and montbretia, and acer leaves follows the shape of the oval frame.*

LEFT *These three designs each use the same flowers and foliage (buttercups, cow parsley and herb Robert) and the same background colour to illustrate three different arrangements in a round frame. The first is a crescent-shaped design which follows the frame outline. The second has a central focal point made up of three main flowers. In the third, the flowers are arranged more naturally as if growing.*

RIGHT *Four ideas are suggested by the rectangular outline of these greetings cards. The first follows half the shape of the frame in an L-shaped design, the largest flower set in the right-angle of the L, and the smaller flowers and dainty foliage softening the outline. On the second card, the focal flower is placed centrally, towards the base of the rectangle, the delicate fern and tiny heuchera leading the eye upwards and outwards. The third card displays a regular design with the pink-edged central daisy claiming immediate attention. The fourth design 'starts' in the top left-hand corner, from where the pendant fuchsias fall to focus attention on the middle of the card. The fuchsia stamens and forget-me-nots then trail away to lead the eye downwards.*

you are looking for ways to suit a design to the shape of its setting.

MAKE A COPY OF A PICTURE YOU ADMIRE

An excellent way of broadening your design experience is to choose an illustration of a flower picture which you particularly like, and to make a 'copy' of it. It will not be an exact copy because your flowers, foliage, stems and so on will not perfectly duplicate those of the original, and because you may well find yourself incorporating ideas of your own. Nevertheless, the exercise can be a valuable one, for if the original has been made by a skilled designer you will, as you make your copy, be learning about the principles of good design in the most practical way possible. In addition, by making your own version of a picture that you admire, you will be well on the way towards developing a style of your own.

Years ago, when I began working with pressed flowers and was at a loss to know how to start design work, I bought a helpful book called *Pressed Flower Decorations* by Margaret Spencer. Deciding that I wanted to try making a 'big picture' for the first time, I looked through the colour plates for a suitable design. It had to be one that I liked, and one for which I had the right sort of pressed material.

I chose the C-shaped design reproduced here. I particularly liked it because of its 'open' quality – each flower in a space of its own – and its use of curving stems. I followed Ms Spencer's advice to find 'a nicely curving stalk to form the outline'. (She suggested that it might be necessary to cut sections from several different stalks to achieve the desired curve.) The next step was to add the main flower with a few smaller flowers arranged around it. The picture was to be completed by 'breaking up the hard line of the main stalk' with the introduction of short curving stems or tendrils, and the final addition of small leaves and flowers 'to fill in and balance the

LEFT *One of my recent designs still showing the influence of Ms Spencer's work. It is in an oval framed backed on velvet. The focal flowers are arranged in groups; the C-shape is reversed; and a butterfly has found its way in.*

TOP *The reproduction of Margaret Spencer's original of which I chose to make a copy.*

design'.

Even when making my first 'copy' I introduced my own variations, working on a fabric background instead of on paper, and placing the largest 'focal' flowers closer to the base of the design. The style was, however, substantially that of Ms Spencer's original, and many of the larger pictures I have made since then show the influence of her work.

LEARN ABOUT BALANCE

Although it is not necessary for a design to be regular in any way, it must be balanced. Balance is not always easy to achieve, and one occasionally looks at a picture, knowing that something is wrong although it is not always clear exactly what. A good technique for diagnosing this sort of problem is to turn the picture round and look at it at a different angle. Quite often, a fault that eluded you when the picture was the right way up becomes glaringly obvious when it is upside-down.

A good exercise in creating balance is to make a picture entirely from leaves. Leaf pictures are more adaptable than flower designs for this 'all ways round' viewing. Try making one and checking its balance from every angle.

You might like to use a similar background to the

one shown here. The leaves are mounted on a mellow plywood which, with its attractive grain, seems to me to be just right for a design made from tree leaves.

MAKE YOUR OWN DESIGNS

If you have followed my suggestions so far, you will realize that at every stage, I have offered the diffident artist something to 'lean' on when making designs: the beauty of a single flower; symmetry; nature as designer; a picture to copy, and so on. But of course, sooner or later, you will want to create something original.

The joy of working with flowers is that you will certainly be able to do this. If you are artist enough to sketch out ideas for designs, either mentally or on paper, so much the better. But if, like me, you are unable to plan in this way, it is still possible to make designs that are both attractive and original. All you have to do is to allow the flowers themselves to make the suggestions. Let me tell you the story of how my favourite – and most successful – picture came about.

Once upon a time I acquired, from the oddments bin of a local art shop, a sturdy plum-coloured mount. I bought it because it was cheap, and although its colour did not immediately inspire me I was sure that I would eventually find a use for it. I took it home and, several weeks later, decided that the obvious flowers to use with it were the similarly-coloured blooms of my hardy fuchsia. At that point, I really had no idea at all about what sort of design I was going to make. I simply placed

ABOVE *Learn about balance. Make a picture entirely from leaves. The three slightly curving clematis stems in this picture suggest lines for the eye to follow. All the other leaves – with their lovely variety of shapes, and spring and autumn colours – fan out from these lines. There is, I hope, some sense of movement, as of leaves lifting in the wind, perhaps, and it is reasonably well-balanced. The picture looks different, but still, I think, effective, if you look at it upside-down. Further acceptable variations can be achieved by viewing either of the two short sides as possible 'tops'.*

ABOVE *Fuchsia tree. 1 Flowers and foliage are placed on a white background.*

ABOVE CENTRE *2 The flowers begin to suggest that they should hang.*

ABOVE *3 The trunk and some leaves are added.*

the mount over some white textured paper on to which I then put the fuchsias. I moved them around with the tip of a soft paintbrush, and waited hopefully for ideas. The first thing the flowers told me, quite clearly, was that they had to hang. That is how they grow, and any attempt to arrange them otherwise looked unnatural. After a while they began, quite by chance, to assume the character of a weeping tree. I arranged them more definitely into this shape, and gave the tree a 'trunk' made from a straightish clematis stem. I then thought I could enhance the weeping effect by using the fuchsias' own slim leaves in the spaces between flowers.

I was pleased with the effect so far. It seemed to be to be stylized and unreal, a bit like an illustration from an eastern fairy-tale. It was obvious that the design needed a base, and I felt that this should be equally stylized, so I chose to make a 'mound' of tiny, intricately-arranged richly-coloured flowers and foliage. I felt that, to fit in with the style of the whole, the mound should be regular in shape, and I therefore drew a light pencil line around the top of a saucer to make an outline within which to work. I then began to build up pieces of thalictrum foliage and heuchera, heather, lady's mantle and forget-me-not flowers. This was done almost like a jigsaw puzzle, fitting in each piece as closely as possible to the next but without the pieces touching or overlapping each other.

I have to admit that when I had finished making this picture, I was delighted with it. The style, I knew, would not be to everybody's taste, but I liked it, and I had the pleasure of knowing that it was my original

LEFT *4 The completed picture.*

ABOVE *A partner for the fuchsia tree (made from pink larkspur and miniature rose leaves).*

design. Of course the truth is that when I began the picture I had no idea how it would turn out. I am therefore grateful to the flowers for showing me what to do, and for liberating the frustrated artist in me.

There is a happy postscript to this story. A year or so after I had begun making 'fuchsia trees', a customer who had bought one of the earliest versions, decided that she would like another picture to make up a pair: the same size, the same colours, the same style, but a different picture. Initially, I was a bit frightened by this request. I knew I should be aiming at a second stylized tree, but at that stage had no further idea what it should look like. I therefore decided to see if the flowers could, once again, come up with some ideas. This time I chose pink larkspur, as having flowers of the right colour, on

which to base the matching picture. And again, as I moved them around, the idea came – this time at the point where they formed themselves into a rough circle which looked vaguely like a standard rose-tree. I picked up this suggestion, and introduced miniature rose leaves with darker pink petals as 'rosebuds'. The fuchsia tree had a partner. And they lived happily ever after!

The point of this story is to prove that there is no need to start with a clear idea of the sort of design you want to make. You can simply take some carefully pressed flowers and foliage, and place them on a background colour that enhances their beauty, inside a frame or mount that suits both flowers and background. Then all you have to do is move them around until they suggest ideas. You will not have to wait for long – for I

RIGHT *In the first of the seed pictures, the tawny owl is fashioned mainly from hogweed seeds, with pear pips (seeds) for eyes, the curved seeds of marigold for 'eyebrows' and cosmos daisies for claws.*

am quite certain that I am not unique in getting some of my best design ideas directly from flowers. Give it a try!

Finally, as a footnote to this section, I should say one more thing. You may be puzzled by the fact that I appear to be flouting my own 'rules' by sticking flowers on a white background and using a mount that keeps them away from the glass. There are, of course, always exceptions to rules, and I have chosen to go on using white paper in this case because its starkness seems to be right for the 'fairy-tale' effect of these pictures, and because experience tells me that small, hardy fuchsias and larkspur are excellent colourkeepers which do not fade and disappear into their background. Also, both these flowers are so sturdy that as long as they are well stuck down, they should not suffer from the lack of direct pressure.

STYLE

There is a sense in which there are as many different styles as there are pressed-flower artists. And the style of even one individual is likely to keep changing and developing as time passes. It is possible, nevertheless, to identify a number of general stylistic areas. You might like to try your hand at each of these.

The modern style in which I work is characterized

LEFT *The fluffy bits of these young great tits consist of the feathery spikelets of grass and reeds.*

by its simplicity and concentration on the individual flower. It often uses only one main flower type in any design, together with one or two smaller species which serve to soften the outline and complement the colour of the main blooms. These designs generally have an 'open' appearance, using space to ensure that the individual beauty of each flower is clearly seen.

In contrast to this, the more traditional style commonly uses a mass of overlapping blooms to create a total effect, rather than focusing attention on individual flowers. Many pictures of this sort contain a large number of different species, and are often big enough to accommodate large specimens. The overall effect of this traditional work is full, heavy and grand.

Representational designs are different again. They can vary greatly, ranging from complex and intricately-worked pictures to 'designs' which seem to present themselves ready-made.

I have seen beautiful examples of complex representational work depicting such subjects as elegant ladies with sumptuous gowns, fashioned entirely from overlapping delphinium petals; graceful swans, brought to life from the feathery silver leaves of cineraria and silverweed; and the most exquisitely-worked landscapes.

Some of the most original representational work I have seen is that which uses seeds in all their subtle varieties of colour, texture and shape to make the most charming and realistic pictures of birds.

185

D E S I G N

LEFT *The two main areas of these jenny-wrens consist of different types of lettuce seeds.*

It is obvious that an enormous amount of loving care has gone into making these pictures. The outline of the bird is first sketched on to the background card, after which the eyes and beak are fixed into position. Then a small area of glue is applied directly to the card and each seed is carefully placed in position, working from the bottom upwards to ensure that the 'feathers' overlap realistically.

It sometimes happens that simple representations of such subjects as butterflies, birds and trees offer themselves straight from the pages of pressing books. A single petal has only to fall from the five-petalled St John's wort – and there is a 'butterfly' with stamen antennae. If two petals fall from the beautifully-veined ballerina geranium, four 'wings' are again revealed (and, if you are lucky, there will also be two visible sections of calyx in the right position for antennae). It is only one step from this to selecting four suitably-proportioned *Clematis montana* leaves, and making a butterfly with an oaty grass spikelet for a body and fuchsia stamens for antennae.

ABOVE **Simple representations of butterflies** *made from (1) the leaves of* Clematis montana, *(2) the veined petals of the ballerina geranium and (3) the petals and stamens of St John's wort.*

187

ABOVE *'Ready-made trees'.*
Green ferns and silver leaves can
conjure up realistic summer and
winter landscapes.

It is not only insects that 'appear' in this way. The aptly-named cranesbill seed-pod simply asks to be made into a bird's head and neck, and looks effective with the feathery leaves of silverweed forming a swan-like body. Other birds 'grow' on my flowering cherry tree. I have only to look at the feathery outlines of its foliage to imagine a group of birds in flight, and those of its leaves which obligingly turn red on one 'breast' in autumn, make delightful robins when given a seed eye, leaf wing and fanciful clematis seed tail.

You will also discover 'trees' in the pages of pressing books. It is a simple matter to incorporate the lush green fern 'species' into summer landscapes, and those with the bare silver 'branches' into wintry scenes. (And whatever the season, a few grass seed 'birds' could fly around the treetops.)

RIGHT *Simply made birds. 1* A
'swan' made from a cranesbill
seed pod and silverweed leaves. 2
A Christmas robin with a cherry
tree body and clematis tail. 3
More cherry leaf birds in flight.

COLOUR

There are three colour elements to be considered in relation to any design: the colour of the flowers; of the

ABOVE ***The choice of background colour.*** *The contrasting effects achieved by mounting buttercups on (**1**) a blending gold background and (**2**) a contrasting blue one.*

background; and of the frame or setting. Vastly different effects can be achieved by different combinations of these three elements. One of the delights of working with flowers is experimenting with them.

Everyone has different ideas on how to choose flower colours. Successful pictures range from those which imitate the summer herbaceous border in presenting a riot of mixed colours, to those which use the most muted of shades (see illustration on page 33). I prefer something between these extremes. I like to use flowers that have retained their original brightness, but usually prefer not to mix too many different flower colours in any one design.

Similar personal preferences will be at work when background colours are chosen. Although I would definitely advise the use of a strong colour when working with flowers that might fade, and suggest that a soft pale green is a good natural-looking background for many designs, I otherwise hesitate to state opinions about what flowers should be used with which background colours. For although I might choose to mount

buttercups, for example, on a blending brown or gold background, you might – quite reasonably – decide they look better on a contrasting blue. Experiment, placing the flowers on different backgrounds to find out which combinations best please you.

Such experiments should continue when you introduce the third element: the frame or setting. Ask yourself what you are looking for – harmony or contrast? And which parts of the picture are you trying to emphasize?

ABOVE LEFT AND RIGHT ***The choice of frame colour.** Look back at the two pictures in the mahogany frames illustrated on pages 57 and 58. Framed as they are there, the colours of the reddish-brown acer leaves in the buttercup picture and the maroon astrantia flowers, are picked up by the frame colour. If the frames are exchanged with gilt ones, as shown here, the buttercup picture suddenly looks altogether lighter, and the flowers become more obvious than the leaves. In the astrantia picture, the small creamy elderflowers are now highlighted. Which frame do you think best suits each picture? There is of course, no wrong or right answer. You must choose the effect that works best for you.*

LEFT AND BELOW LEFT *The designs on the lids of these coloured porcelain boxes are fairly similar, but each one is mounted on a different-coloured fabric to match the base of the box. Quite different effects can be achieved by interchanging the lids. In the lower picture the pink lid has been exchanged with the green one. Now the green foliage on the pink velvet is highlighted by its new green base, and the pink heather florets on the green background come to life because of the pink underneath them.*

RIGHT AND BELOW RIGHT
Similar changes in perception of colour take place when the lids of these two boxes are interchanged. Which is the better, the matching or contrasting effect? It is a purely personal choice.

CHAPTER FIVE

Presentation

HE traditional setting for a pressed-flower design is a picture frame. Ten years ago you would probably have presented your work in this form, or possibly as one of a number of smaller items, the settings for which might well have been improvised. Pictures are still, of course, one of the most effective and versatile methods of presentation, and there is always room for imaginative improvisation, especially when working with children. We are fortunate today, however, in being able to buy an enormous variety of attractive settings specifically designed for craft work. And even this most traditional of crafts is now being influenced by the introduction of modern techniques and materials.

This chapter aims to present a guide to the main ways of presenting designs. It starts with the very simplest and inexpensive suggestions for use by complete beginners and children in schools and progresses through ideas for designs protected by varnish and covering film, to the range of settings to be purchased from craft suppliers. It continues with the relatively new technique of encapsulating flowers in resin and includes a consideration of different approaches to framing a traditional pressed flower picture. The final section is on presentations for special occasions.

IDEAS FOR CHILDREN

Making designs from flowers and leaves which they have pressed themselves can be a satisfying and pleasurable activity for children. It may not always be easy, however, for teachers to find suitable methods of presentation, attractive, and yet, at the same time, inexpensive and simple enough for the children to handle without too much adult help. In the interests of economy and simplicity, therefore, I suggest that, when working with young children, the 'rule' that pressed-flower designs must always be protected is abandoned.

Unprotected designs may not last very long, but they give real pleasure during the making. And with the right sort of flowers and 'settings', they should survive the perilous journey home, and last quite long enough to give pleasure to families and friends.

Many flowers serve admirably for unprotected

RIGHT *Ribbon bookmarks protected with a manageably small area of covering film.*

ABOVE *A leaf calendar, the design for which was assembled quickly and confidently by an assured young artist.*

FAR RIGHT *A simple, sturdy heather calendar. The design is outlined in blue felt tip pen.*

work, including the wild buttercups, daisies, cow parsley and heather, and the cultivated larkspur, astrantia, montbretia and fuchsia. Special consideration may be given to the everlasting varieties here, because they are particularly sturdy; you may be able to make a virtue of necessity and use such flowers as the bulky helichrysum (strawflower or yellow paper daisy) which is unsuitable for use in protected designs.

Almost any foliage will do, as long as it is not too fine or, as in the case of autumn leaves, too brittle. Include a variety of wild grasses and sturdy seed-pods in the list of plant materials to collect.

If the children are short of ideas on design, try them on the various possibilities suggested in Chapter 4 in the section on frame shapes. My experience of children, however, indicates that they have fewer inhibitions than adults in making designs, and soon have a clear idea of exactly what they want to do. (My own young artist assembled his design on the illustrated leaf calendar with an enviable speed and assurance. He then completely refused to listen to my suggestion that the top leaves were a little large in proportion to those in the delicate pattern beneath. That was how he liked it, he said, and that was how it was going to stay!)

It is a good idea to suggest to the children that they lay out their whole design on their chosen background before sticking anything down.

You will need to find a suitable adhesive that can be applied in small spots. It is a good idea to decant small quantities of this on to flat dishes for ease of application. The best applicators are like cocktail sticks.

The sticking stage is an important one for unprotected designs. Children should be advised that too much glue will spoil their work, but too little could also put it at risk. It is therefore necessary to use more than the single spot recommended for protected work. Several tiny spots should be applied to the back of each item, which should then be carefully and firmly smoothed down.

CHILDREN'S CALENDARS

Acquire some pieces of sturdy card, preferably in varying colours, and cut them to a variety of different sizes. (Try asking the local printer or art shop for offcuts.) Ask the children to spread out their pressed material, and to select a background suitable for the design they intend. If they are capable of line work, suggest that they use a coloured felt-tip pen and ruler to outline their design area, as on the heather calendar. Once the design is complete, it is a simple matter to attach a calendar booklet and a 'hanger' made from a loop of ribbon, with some good adhesive tape.

Calendar

PAPER PLATE PICTURES

The paper plate has several advantages as a method of presenting pictures. It allows children to work within a circular outline for a change, and the plate rim serves as an attractive frame for the picture and gives it some protection. Moreover, paper plates are now available in a variety of interesting colours. The best means of hanging such a picture is probably to attach a small curtain ring to the back of it by means of a short length of ribbon and some adhesive tape.

197

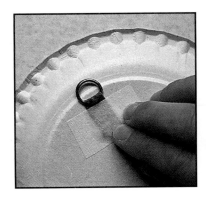

LEFT *Paper plate pictures made from flowers which are sturdy enough to remain unprotected: buttercups, daisies, larkspur and anaphalis.*

ABOVE *Prepare a paper plate picture for hanging by attaching a small curtain ring to its back with a short length of ribbon and some adhesive tape.*

LEFT *The supermarket tray is a good alternative to the paper plate as a setting for an unprotected picture. Its depth makes it particularly suitable for use with the more bulky ever-lasting flowers like helichrysum and with such attractive seed pods as those of montbretia.*

SUPERMARKET TRAYS AS PICTURE FRAMES

A good alternative to the paper plate is the sort of flat container used by many supermarkets for packaging meat. If you can collect enough (well-washed!) trays like this, they make attractive settings for flower work. Children may find it difficult to work within their fairly deep recesses. If this is the case, make the task easier — and the finished effect more interesting — by cutting a piece of sturdy coloured paper to the size of the inside of the base. The design should be stuck on to this paper, which can then be carefully glued into the tray. A bonus point for this type of setting is that it can quite easily be covered with 'cling film' (plastic wrap). This ensures a longer, more dust-free life. Use a curtain ring 'hanger' as on the paper plate.

BOOKMARKS

These can be made of thin card, cut to a suitable shape. If you have a means of cutting an attractive deckled edge, or if your artists are able to outline the card, so much the better, but neither of these processes is essential. The role of bookmark should be a perfect one for a pressed flower design: for if it is used for its intended purpose, it remains pressed flat within a protective

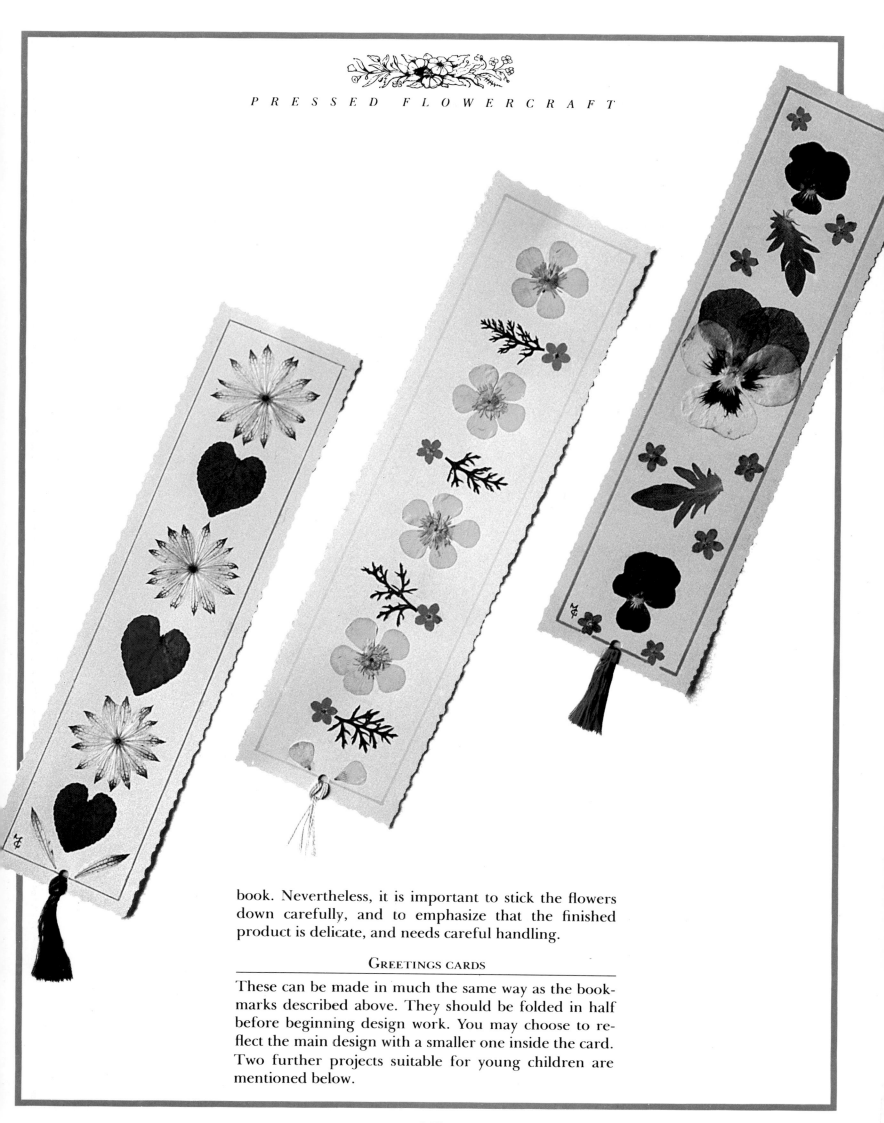

book. Nevertheless, it is important to stick the flowers down carefully, and to emphasize that the finished product is delicate, and needs careful handling.

GREETINGS CARDS

These can be made in much the same way as the bookmarks described above. They should be folded in half before beginning design work. You may choose to reflect the main design with a smaller one inside the card. Two further projects suitable for young children are mentioned below.

LEFT **Unprotected bookmarks.**
*These simple and attractive
designs were made with astrantia,
buttercups and pansies each of
which was carefully stuck down
with several tiny areas of glue.*

ABOVE *These unprotected
greetings cards are made in a
similar way to the bookmarks. The
pictures include saxifrage,
buttercups and astrantia. Note
how they can be made even more
charming by the addition of a
small design inside the card
which reflects the main design.*

LEAF PRINTS

These constitute an attractive way of using pressed
leaves, particularly those with an interesting outline or
prominent veins. You will need coloured ink or paint,
and soft brushes.

Some experiments will probably be necessary
before you find the right sort of paper to use as background, and the best printing medium. I use ordinary
ink in a variety of colours. This may need diluting
slightly with water, and generally also requires the
addition of one or two drops of dishwashing liquid so
that the ink will wet the leaves' surface adequately.

Children will be able to choose whether to use a
single leaf type or several varieties in any one picture.
They may also like to mix real leaves and leaf prints, as
in the beech leaf design.

SPRAYED CHRISTMAS CARDS

A variety of attractive cards can be simply made by this
method. Collect and press seasonal foliage, such as holly,
ivy and some obligingly Christmas-tree-shaped fern. (If
you had the foresight to collect young holly leaves, they
may be flexible enough to be pressed in the traditional

TOP ***Leaf prints 1*** *Brush ink sparingly onto the more textured side of the leaf.*

ABOVE ***3*** *Remove the leaf, taking great care not to cause any smudging.*

way, but I have to admit to having ironed mine to flatten them!) Also needed are silver spray and sturdy red paper, cut out and folded into cards.

First, place one or more pieces of pressed foliage on to the card. (It is a good idea to hold them temporarily in place with a tiny piece of flat plasticine so that they do not move during the spraying.) Then lightly spray the card and leaves. After the removal of the sprayed leaves, you have three separate elements from which to make up designs: silver leaves, green leaves (reverse sides) and leaf 'negatives', outlined in silver on the red background.

OTHER INEXPENSIVE IDEAS

I am including the following suggestions because they are relatively inexpensive and might therefore be considered suitable projects for older children or inexperienced adults. The settings described below are all protected in some way and there is no reason why the experienced pressed-flower designer should not use them for more advanced work.

TOP ***2*** *Place the leaf, ink-side down onto the background. Cover it with a piece of blotting paper or kitchen tissue before pressing it down firmly and evenly.*

ABOVE ***4*** *The same leaf may be used several times.*

TOP RIGHT *A beech leaf print incorporating the real leaves from which the prints were made.*

RIGHT *Sprayed Christmas cards made from three separate elements: pressed green leaves, sprayed silver leaves and the 'negative' silhouettes made by the removal or repositioning of the sprayed leaves.*

ABOVE *Pebble paperweights.*
Simple designs of lobelia and
larkspur have been varnished
onto these pebbles.

PROTECTION WITH VARNISH

Ordinary household varnish is a good means of protection, provided that a suitable background is selected and the right pressed material used. The range of possible flowers for this work is somewhat limited because they must be neither too thick for the varnish to seal them effectively nor so fine that they 'disappear' into their protective coating. Most of the flowers previously recommended for unprotected work can be used with this technique. The illustrations in this section show that love-in-a-mist (devil-in-a-bush) and lobelia are also good subjects.

The background should be smooth and not too absorbent – stone, wood, cork and wax are all possibilities (see below). The technique for applying varnish and flowers is the same in each case: prepare the surface of the background, making sure it is smooth, clean and dust-free; plan the design by placing the flowers on to the background in the positions they will eventually take up; transfer this design to a temporary surface while applying the first, thin coat of varnish; then, while the varnish is still wet, position the flowers in it. (There is, of

ABOVE *These wall plaques have been cut from the thinnest possible plywood. They were scorched around the edge to make an attractive outline before designs made with montbretia, heather and fuchsia were varnished on.*

course, no need to use any glue – a great advantage of this procedure is that, for the first 15 minutes or so, it is possible to use a cocktail stick to move the flowers around in the fluid varnish, until they are perfectly positioned.) The design should then be allowed to dry for at least eight hours in a dust-free place, before the second protective coat is applied.

PEBBLE PAPERWEIGHTS The first requirement is of course to find some suitable stones. The large, smooth, flattish seashore pebbles are ideal – look for those with the most interesting shapes and colours. It is a good idea to examine them while they are still wet, for although a beautiful glistening pebble often dries to a more non-descript appearance, the subtle colour variations will re-appear when the varnish is applied.

WOODEN WALL PLAQUES Woods have so many different colours and grain patterns that it should be easy to find suitable pieces. The simplest and cheapest way of acquiring these is to buy offcuts of plywood. The appropriate size and shape depend very much on the

BELOW *Cork-mat wall plaques with a varnished design of buttercups and cow parsley.*

nature of the intended design; make sure that the surface and edges are smooth. In the examples shown here, I have used plywood so thin that it can be cut to attractive shapes with scissors. (To finish off the edge in an interesting way, I have outlined the shape by scorching it in the flame of my gas cooker.) Lightweight plaques can be made to hang in the same way as paper plate pictures, whereas the heavier ones need hooks attached with screws.

CORK PLAQUES Cork makes an attractive and interesting background, and is easily obtainable in the form of square wall tiles or round table-mats. Use bright flowers so that they stand out against the strong colour of the cork. Hang by the curtain-ring and ribbon method.

CANDLES Candles decorated with flowers look lovely, although I have never been quite sure whether they are actually intended for use, or just as ornaments. I remember once burning a pressed flower candle I had bought, and being very upset to see the flowers literally going up in smoke. I have since devised two methods of

RIGHT *Two candles adorned with pressed flowers. Both the lobelia on the conical candle and the love-in-a-mist on the square one have been varnished on.*

getting round this problem. One is to use candles so fat that they burn down inside, leaving the flowers intact. The other is to apply the decoration only to the base. The best solution of all is to make the design so attractive that nobody even thinks of using the candle!

Candles of any colour may be used, and the design varnished on exactly as described above. (An alternative method, for those who have made their own candles, is to leave them in a warm place until the wax softens a little and then press in the flowers; finally, holding the candles by their wicks, dip them lightly in molten wax to seal the flowers.

SELF-ADHESIVE FILM AS A MEANS OF PROTECTION

Clear self-adhesive covering film is one of the most versatile ways of protecting flower designs. It serves to protect the bookmarks, cards and lampshades described below, and can equally well cover designs on folders, matchboxes or decorative mats. It can even be used instead of glass on small pictures.

Film has the advantages of being relatively inexpensive and easily obtainable (although I have to

admit to preferring the less widely available type, with the matt finish, to the shiny-surfaced type which is sold for book covering at most large stationers). The shiny film, though just as good as a protector, tends to show up any imperfections more than the matt version.

Applying self-adhesive film well is quite a skilled operation, and you will need to practise on 'designs' that do not matter, for you will be very disappointed if a successful piece of work, on which you have spent a long time, is ruined by the faulty application of film.

Film that is well applied should be almost unnoticeable and therefore used to cover only relatively flat subjects. Any particularly thick specimens – like heather, for example – will cause bubbles or blisters.

BELOW *1 Applying clear self-adhesive film to protect a design.*

BELOW *2 The film should be cut to a slightly larger size than the design and then trimmed after application.*

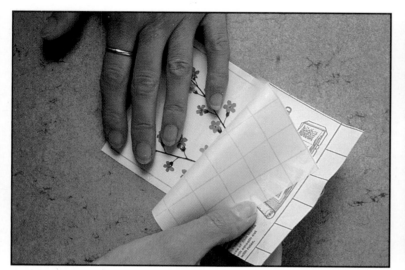

Some of the most common blemishes on work covered in this way are finger-prints, which appear on the sticky side of the film (and are therefore impossible to remove after its application). Similar problems are caused by tiny bits of unwanted plant material, dust, grit, or hair which have a tendency to appear underneath the film on the design surface. To counteract such problems, keep your hands scrupulously clean and, if possible, avoid touching the sticky side of the film altogether. Secondly, try to work in perfectly dust-free conditions, taking care to see that the surface of your design in particular is absolutely clean.

Static electricity can be a problem. It manifests itself when you are applying the film, causing petals to rise up to meet it as it comes down. They may then become folded over or end up in the wrong position.

You can counter the effects of static in several ways. Try to avoid working with this covering on very dry days; damp or humid conditions are preferable. Introduce temporary 'humidity', by breathing gently on the design just before you apply the film. Stick down every item in your design – it seems a shame to have to

do this when it will soon be held down quite securely anyway, but this procedure will, at least, prevent whole flowers from jumping up to attach themselves to the film prematurely. Peel off only the top half inch (1cm) of film from its protective backing; stick this adhesive strip over the top of the design area. Then, very gradually, peel the backing from a small area at a time, smoothing down the newly exposed sticky surface with your free hand.

It is generally a good idea to cut the film out to a size slightly larger than the design area, and to trim off the surplus after application. The top strip must be properly aligned: if it is not, the film at the bottom may miss part of the design altogether.

BELOW *Greetings cards with design insets. These look attractive and provide good practice if you are using covering film for the first time. (The design area is much smaller than that of the plain covered cards illustrated.) A professional finish is given by outlining the insets with a fine double black line.*

BELOW *Cards with the whole surface area covered with film. The ornamental gilt outline was drawn before covering.*

BOOKMARKS

Introduce yourself to using film by making items that have only very small areas to be covered. Ribbon bookmarks are an excellent way to start. They each require a piece of stiff ribbon about 15 in (38 cm) long. This is folded in half and trimmed at the end to an attractive shape. The flower design is then stuck on and the film applied by the method described.

GREETINGS CARDS

Blank cards tend to be expensive and are usually only white or cream. The 'cards' shown are made on good-quality textured writing paper. This is available in a wide range of colours, all with matching envelopes. Paper about 8½ × 5½ in (21 × 14 cm) folds in two to make an ideal card.

RIGHT *A lampshade design for a cylindrical shade. The design is best made while the background is still in a flat strip.*

RIGHT **Mirror making.** *A mirror design on a paper circle and a similar design made up into a mirror.*

FAR RIGHT *Four more simple mirror designs.*

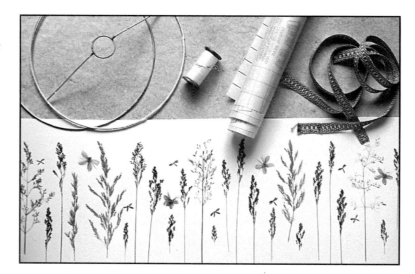

You might like to start by making cards with design insets. This makes the covering process simpler (the inset area being only about one-third of the whole card). It also looks extremely attractive. Cut the inset card to suitable proportions, decorate it with a flower design, and cover it, using a piece of film of slightly larger dimensions, trimming off the surplus after covering. The protected design should then be stuck to the coloured card. For a professional finish, the inset should be carefully outlined, using a fine-tipped pen and ruler. A double outline looks particularly good.

When you are satisfied with your covering technique, you may wish to make designs directly on to the coloured card. If a decorative outline is to be drawn round the work, it is probably best done before starting the design. This time the film should cover the whole surface of the card.

LAMPSHADES The only reason lampshades are in this section at all is that the method I use to cover them is the application of self-adhesive film. Otherwise, they are perhaps out of place in a beginners' section. Indeed, some pressed-flower experts make only lampshades.

There are many types of shade, but a simple one may be made as follows: buy from a craft shop a pair of lampshade rings and some plain, pale-coloured shade-covering material. I suggest that you begin with a regular cylindrical shade, and do the design work while the background is still in a flat strip.

Remember that the flowers will be silhouetted when the lamp is on, so the emphasis should be as much on shape as on colour. Grasses are well proportioned for this setting, and are delicate and attractive enough to stand on their own. Alternatively, designs consisting only of leaves such as those of *Acer* or herb Robert work just as well. A mixed design of flowers and foliage is perhaps the prettiest of all.

The covering stage is the difficult one, for a large area of film is involved. But starting from one short side, and peeling off a little of the protective backing at a time, it should be possible to apply it smoothly. Next, encircle the rings with your design strip; glue the join; glue or stitch the shade to the rings; and finish if off with a border of decorative braid at the top and bottom.

These shades can look very beautiful, and both flowers and film last surprisingly well. It is advisable, however, to use rings of at least 7 in (18 cm) in diameter, and a light bulb no more powerful than 60W.

There are two further techniques that use a clear protective film, but they require special equipment.

HEAT SEALING

This modern technique works well on pressed-flower designs, which are permanently protected by the plastic coating applied during the process. Most towns have an art- or 'copy-shop' which should do the job for you.

BADGE AND MIRROR MAKING

This is a lovely and inexpensive way of turning simple flower designs into something decorative or useful. The design is made on a circle of coloured paper, leaving a border of about ½ in (1 cm) all the way round, to allow for folding under. (The circles for the mirror illustrated here have a diameter of 3 in (7.5 cm) with an artwork diameter of 2 in (5 cm).) The design goes through a badge-making machine to have its protective cover and badge or mirror fitting fixed into place. Some schools and clubs are lucky enough to own such a machine.

P U R C H A S E D   S E T T I N G S

Imaginative craft suppliers are offering an ever-widening variety of settings in which work can be mounted. These range from small, relatively inexpensive items, like pendants and pill boxes, to some special products such as individually-turned wooden bowls and hand-cut lead crystal jars, for favourite designs or special gifts.

These purchased items have four great advantages: they are usually round or oval – the ideal shapes for flower work; they can generally be assembled quickly

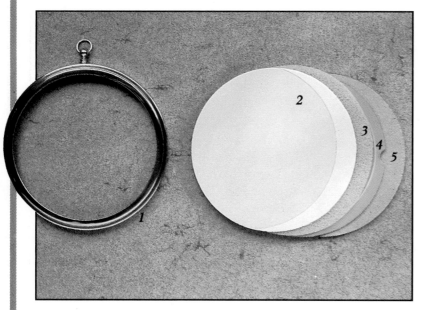

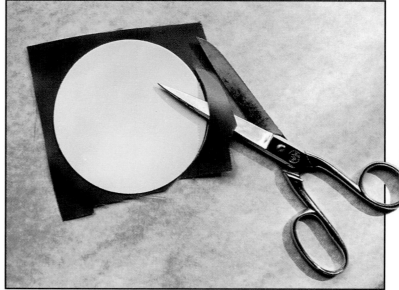

ABOVE *The main components of settings are* **1** *A frame or lid rim* **2** *A sturdy protective covering made of acetate (glass is an alternative for many items, but I actually prefer acetate as it is light and unbreakable) – both advantages if gifts are to be posted. Moreover, when the whole setting is locked together, the acetate assumes a slightly convex shape which looks attractive, and keeps the flowers under firm pressure)* **3** *A layer of sponge* **4** *A locking plate (not in most pendants), which with the sponge padding holds the assembly securely together and ensures that, with the exclusion of all air, the flowers remain in good condition* **5** *A piece of thick flock-backed card for frames or thin flock-backed liner for lids.*

and easily, leaving more time to concentrate on designs; they are, for the most part, well made so that good flower work mounted in them has a really professional appearance; and finally, when presented as gifts, they are more than just flower designs: they are attractive in themselves and, in many cases, useful.

The components and assembly procedures for the settings described below are common to most of them, and can usefully be dealt with in a general introduction.

☛ First prepare the design background. This is simple if the work is to be mounted directly on to the manufacturer's design card. I prefer to use a fabric background because of the range of colours and textures available. I therefore use the design card simply as a template around which to cut my material (usually velvet or satin). Before cutting out, it is advisable to back the fabric with a self-adhesive covering material (clear or patterned – it will not show). This gives it more body and makes it generally easier to handle.

☛ Then make the design. This should suit the shape of the frame and the purpose for which it is intended. (The lid of a mahogany box made for a man's study, for

ABOVE *Prepare the design background by cutting out the fabric (backed with a self-adhesive covering material), using the manufacturer's design card as a template.*

example, should have an altogether stronger, less delicate design than that of a pink porcelain pot, designed for a woman's dressing table.)

I think it important in pressed-flower work in general, and in these dainty settings in particular, that there should be a good border between the outline of the design and the edge of the frame. (Nothing looks more haphazard than badly positioned flowers disappearing under the frame edge.) A good way to ensure a regular border is to make your design with the frame actually fitted around the background while you are working.

It is necessary to stick down each item because although the assembly will eventually hold the flowers firmly in place, it is almost impossible to transfer unfixed work into a setting without disturbing some of the components.

☛ Before assembling your work, ensure that the finished design is free from unwanted 'bits' of any sort.

Clean the acetate carefully. This is best done with an anti-static cloth. For good measure, breathe gently on to both acetate and design immediately before assembly.

ABOVE *Ensure a regular border around your work by making the design with the background actually fitted inside the frame.*

RIGHT *Use firm thumb pressure to ensure that the locking plate is pushed firmly home. This is an important process in the assembly of these settings.*

Place the acetate in the frame, and the design, face downards, against it.

Place the sponge padding in position, and then insert the locking plate, raised side towards the design. Firm thumb pressure is needed all round the perimeter to push this firmly home.

Insert the thick flock-backed card into the frame, or lid liner into the lid. The liner should be held in position with adhesive or some double-sided sticky tape.

214

LEFT *Pendants come in a variety of sizes from the small and dainty to the large and bold. Choose flowers and designs that best suit frame, size and shape. The small circular frames use heuchera, cow parsley and forget-me-nots; the small ovals, spearwort, heuchera and heather; and the larger ovals, anaphalis, cow parsley and heather.*

PENDANTS, BROOCHES AND KEY RINGS

When I first purchased pendant settings about eight years ago, I had two to choose from. The present choice of at least 22, in a variety of shapes, sizes and materials allows far greater flexibility.

Each one is available in a gold- or silver-plated finish and can be hung on a chain to make a pendant or on a bow to make a fob-brooch. Some designs are now available with pins on the back to make pin-on brooches, and any frame can be converted into a key-ring by the addition of a simple fitting. They are sold with instructions for assembly, which is a simple affair similar to the procedure described above except that, instead of being held in by a locking plate, the design is secured by three small tabs which fold inwards from the edge of the frame.

The smallest of these settings will be a real challenge to your delicacy of touch, ingenuity as a designer, and ability to find flowers and foliage small enough for the purpose. My most valued stand-bys for such tiny designs are heuchera, forget-me-not, anaphalis (pearly everlasting), spearwort, cow parsley and heather, and I am always on the look-out for unusually small specimens of other flowers like heartsease (wild pansy), celandines or daisies. The 'growing flower' design is usually the best in these very small settings. Try using one main specimen of something like anaphalis embellished with tiny florets of heather, or three or more flowers of small subjects like forget-me-nots or heuchera.

ABOVE ***Transparent pendants.*** *(1½ in (3.8 cm) in diameter.) The flowers are **1** love-in-a-mist **2** wild carrot **3** astrantia **4** heuchera.*

Larger pendant frames permit the introduction of many more and different flowers, increasing the scope for design. Crescent-shapes or posy arrangements can be made from a group of tiny flowers, and lovely 'growing' designs, using just one or two larger specimens like snowdrops, or even such unlikely subjects as the side-shoots of montbretia are possible. Remember also the 'start small, start simple' section of Chapter 4: a pendant is an excellent setting for one perfect flower.

There is one further adaptation of which these pendant fittings are capable. If a second piece of sturdy acetate is substituted for backing card, attractive see-through designs become possible. These are especially useful for flowers like the wild carrot, which has an equally attractive top and underside. Or two intricate flowers like astrantia may be positioned back to back. Using two slightly different specimens may give added interest to a design. An advantage of this method of presentation is that it will certainly match the wearer's clothing, which will show through, and become the design background.

ABOVE *Pill-box and ashtray designs ranging from the simplest single flower like the astrantia **1** through designs which add embellishment to one main flower **2** daisy and **3** heartsease; to the delicate crescent arrangement of forget-me-nots and London Pride **4** and the intricate design of lobelia, heuchera and alchemilla **5**.*

PILL-BOXES AND PERSONAL ASH-TRAYS

These miniature boxes are convenient for carrying in a handbag. They are made from gilding metal and have hinged lids, the designs for which should be assembled exactly as in the general instructions given previously. The pill-box has a white plastic liner, and the ash-tray an extending cigarette rest.

The design area, like that of the medium- and large-sized pendants, offers considerable scope for flower choice and design shape, ranging from the simple use of a single perfect flower to an intricate design of tiny specimens.

PICTURE FRAMES

When picture frames are mentioned, one normally thinks of relatively large, rectangular wooden settings. Such traditional frames are fully dealt with later in this chapter, but they are so different from the delicate gilding metal or silver-plated frames under consideration here that they might just as well be thought of as a different setting altogether.

These small frames, with their watch-top hangers and their lovely round and oval shapes, have such character that they could only enhance a good design. An enormous variety of flowers and design shapes can be used in these frames, and widely different effects can be achieved by the use of different background fabrics and colours. A velvet backing, for example, pressed firmly around the edges by a locking plate, produces an interesting graduation of colour from the edge to the middle of the picture (see illustration on page 12).

Since people may prefer to hang such small pictures in pairs or groups, you may decide to make matching designs, using harmonious combinations of flowers, shapes, and backgrounds. (See illustrations for ideas.)

HANDBAG MIRRORS

These 3in (7.5cm) diameter mirrors, sold in protective pouchettes, make useful and attractive personal gifts. Assemble your setting according to instructions, up to the point at which the locking plate is secured. Then press in the gilt-rimmed mirror-fitting supplied.

TRINKET BOXES

These are available in both gilding metal and silver-plate, with lid diameters of either 3 in (7.5 cm) or 4 in (10 cm). They all have small feet and vacuum-formed flock liners. The gilt boxes have bodies with a satin finish and shiny lid rims, and the larger of the two can also be bought as a sewing kit with a compartmentalised flock insert that could equally well serve for rings or ear-studs. The 4in (10cm) silver-plated box can be purchased either as a large trinket box or as a dusting bowl with a white interior and powder-puff.

Because the silver-plated items are a little more expensive than the gilt ones, I tend to use them with my most intricate designs. Silver plate also looks particularly good with pink or blue flowers and backgrounds.

For a special gift, try making a matching picture and trinket box, using one of your favourite designs.

PORCELAIN BOXES

For anyone interested in working with colour combinations, these boxes are a must. (Some of the larger round boxes were illustrated in the section on colour at the end

FAR LEFT *Four simple heather designs illustrating the size and shape of four of the most useful gilding metal frames available. These ovals measure **a)** and **b)** respectively 4½ in (11.5 cm) × 3½ in (8.9 cm) and 3¾ in (9.5 cm) × 2½ in (6.1 cm). The round frames **c)** and **d)** respectively are 3 in (7 cm) and 4 in (10.2 cm) in diameter.*

LEFT *Three harmonizing larkspur pictures in a range of pinks and blues.*

TOP **Handbag mirrors.** *These offer an even greater scope for design than the small circular pictures they resemble. Whereas the phlox and heuchera design* (**centre**) *would look equally good as a hanging picture, the symmetrical anaphalis design* (**right**) *might be too formal for*

of Chapter 4.) They are sold in a variety of sizes, round and oval, and in a choice of colours. They are all presented in attractive satin-lined boxes with matching or contrasting linings.

Choosing colours is a fascinating and complex process. It is a question of deciding how best to mix and match the colours of the flowers, background, porcelain base and presentation box-lining.

The small round boxes (1½ in (3.2 cm) in diameter) shown, illustrate simple, single flower designs, whereas the little ovals (2 in (5 cm) × 1½ in (3.8 cm)) display more intricate 'posies'. Similar designs look quite different on backgrounds and bases of different colours.

HAND-TURNED WOODEN BOWLS

These individually-made items are inevitably at the expensive end of the range. But, with their dark mahogany or light elm bases, they are naturally beautiful and offer an opportunity to adapt your designs to blend with the subtle colours of wood.

such a setting. This regular design is, however, ideal for a mirror setting.

TOP *A 4 in (10 cm) gilt box containing a sewing kit. The simple lid design shows love-in-a-mist on a blue velvet background.*

ABOVE LEFT *Pink and blue designs look particularly good in silver-plated settings such as these 3 in (7.5 cm) trinket boxes. These designs are made with daisies and forget-me-nots on pink velvet, rock roses and heuchera on pale satin and burnet saxifrage on royal blue velvet.*

ABOVE *A matching silver-plated trinket box and oval frame each showing a highly intricate design of lobelia, heuchera and alchemilla.*

HAND-CUT LEAD CRYSTAL JARS

These are some of the latest and most expensive additions to the range of purchased settings, and their beautiful lead crystal bases and silver-plated lid rims demand the very best designs.

There are two other useful and relatively inexpensive items in this range of purchased settings which are worth a mention. Their assembly procedure is quite different from those referred to earlier.

PAPERWEIGHTS

These are both pretty and practical as settings for pressed flower designs.

Preparation and assembly procedures are the same for each shape. First prepare the design background. This stage is important because, unlike all the frames mentioned so far, the paperweight setting does not mask the edge of the background. If you are using fabric – and I certainly still prefer to do so – back it with a self-adhesive film to prevent any fraying round the edge and cut it out neatly. The design should be made in the usual way – but remember that the whole area of the

LEFT ABOVE *Three small oval porcelain pots with delicate 'posy' designs. Flowers and background colours were chosen to blend with the colours of the bases.*

ABOVE *Five small round porcelain pots, each with a single love-in-a-mist forming its own 'design'. The background colour is chosen in each case to match the colour of the base. It is interesting to note that similar flowers can look quite different when mounted on different backgrounds.*

LEFT *Hand-turned wooden bowls. 1 The 1 in (2.5 cm) diameter designs are based on a single daisy and three spearwort. 2 The 4 in (10 cm) bowl has a phlox and heuchera design. 3 On the 3 in (7.5 cm) bowls, buttercups were chosen to blend with the light base and three beautiful specimens of geum pick up the colour of their mahogany base.*

background will be visible, and that the border left around the edge could therefore be narrower. Stick down each item and place the completed design, face downwards, into the recess. Finally, peel off the protective backing from the self-adhesive baize provided and stick it firmly on to the base of the paperweight. It may seem surprising, but this is quite sufficient to hold the whole assembly securely together.

DOOR FINGER-PLATES

These are coming back into fashion and look beautiful when adorned with pressed flowers which have been chosen to complement the decor of the room for which they are intended. They are an interesting shape, long and narrow, and call for a special type of design. I like to use tall subjects like montbretia spikes or grasses, or a group of flowers, with the largest at the bottom and the smaller, lighter specimens leading the eye upwards.

This setting, however, demands more skill than most because only the clear plastic plate is supplied. You must provide the design background, the means to hold it in place, and the screws to fix the plate to the door.

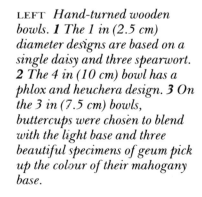

ABOVE *Hand-cut lead crystal jars. The first design uses the pointed bracts of astrantia which seem to me to reflect the pattern cut in the glass. They are mounted on a silvery-green background to blend with the crystal. The second jar has a design on a rich blue velvet background.*

I use sturdy card in a variety of suitable colours as background. This must be cut with a craft knife to fit snugly into the recess. The main difficulty is making holes through the card in exactly the right places to match up with the projecting screw holes on the plate: the best solution is to mark the position of these holes and then cut them out, preferably with a hole punch. Once the design is complete and in position, it can be held in place with a backing of self-adhesive baize.

ABOVE *Cast glass paperweights. The beautiful flower-shaped ones are decorated with anaphalis; the useful oval shapes show heartsease and phlox designs; and the small round one has a central specimen of narcissus, soleil d'or.*

SETTING FLOWERS IN RESIN

Before starting resin work, you will need to acquire some different materials and settings and learn a few new techniques. It is well worth while because it can greatly increase the number of ways in which you can present your designs. Above all, flowers can be mounted in smaller settings than would otherwise be possible.

I began working with resin because I wanted to make ear-studs and rings. The results of my early efforts were so encouraging, that I soon widened my range to include other tiny items: small stick-pins, dainty

LEFT *Examples of designs suitable for the long narrow shape of door finger plates. In the first, the pendant fuchsias hang down its length. Both the larkspur of the second design and the celandines of the third lead the eye upwards from the large specimens at the base towards the smaller ones at the top.*

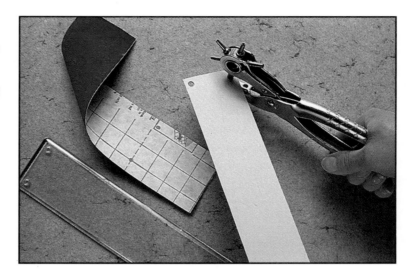

LEFT *Mark the position of the holes to be made in the card and cut them with a hole punch.*

bangles on silver-plated wires, and cuff-links. As well as using new settings, I was pleased with the new effects that working with resin enabled me to achieve. (I remember being particularly delighted when I first used the bright red bells of heuchera, and then sky-blue forget-me-nots, on a pure white background. The resulting 'pictures' looked like intricate enamel-work or delicate painting on porcelain.) It was at this point that I decided to introduce two more resin items, this time duplicating settings I had already used in the more conventional 'take-apart' form – pendants and brooches. These have proved popular because of their delicate appearance.

To set flowers in resin, the following materials and equipment are required:

MATERIALS

A range of jewellery components in which to set your work. These should all have an upstanding edge of $1/32$-$1/16$ in (0.1-0.2 cm) to prevent the resin from flowing away. Suitable components are available in many shapes, sizes and materials. (These include silver and gold-plated metals and also pure silver and gold.)

Devices for keeping components level. Any item into which resin is going to be poured must be perfectly flat. This is not difficult to achieve in the case of such flat components as bangle-tops and pendant 'cups' – but for any item with a projecting back a method of keeping it level has to be devised. For ear-studs, for example, with their projecting 'posts', I use a piece of stripboard (the material normally used for assembling electrical circuits) because it has a large number of regularly-spaced holes through which the posts can conveniently slot. The only preparation it needs is to be supported at both ends with a strip of wood measuring about $1/2$ in (1 cm) square.

Resin. I use a one-to-one pour-on coating resin. This comes in two bottles, and is prepared for use by

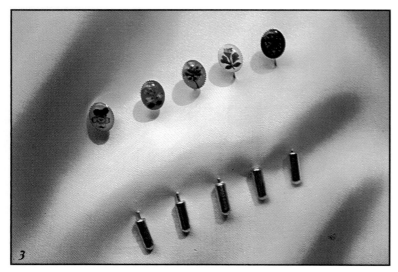

*1 Sterling silver ear studs made with tiny flowers set in resin. 2 Dainty flower designs in silver-plated rings. 3 Small stick pins with a range of delicate flower designs. Note that the blue one (**left**) is made with a tiny specimen of heartsease, measuring less than ¼ in (0.6 cm) across. 4 Dainty bangles with single or triple design areas on silver-plated wires.*

mixing together exactly equal quantities from each.

A means of measuring exact amounts of resin. It is possible simply to use the bottle tops to add a 'capful' of each resin to your mixing container. In the interests of precision, however, I use plastic hypodermic syringes. **NB Do not allow children to use hypodermic syringes as they can be very dangerous.**

A series of colour pastes to create background colours. An initial range might include white, black, red, green and royal blue.

Containers for mixing resins. These should have smooth flat surfaces and be dust-free.

A mixing stick. This should have a flat straight edge to ensure the thorough mixing of the two resins. A small wooden lollipop stick is ideal.

Cocktail sticks for applying tiny quantities of resin to small jewellery components.

A fine soft brush for applying the top coat of clear resin.

A curing cabinet (optional). This ensures that the resin cures quickly, at a constant warm temperature, and in dust-free conditions. Mine is a small store-

TOP *As components increase in size (these pendants are ³⁄₄in (1.8 cm) high, it is possible to introduce slightly larger flowers. Used here is a spray of heuchera, heartsease, anaphalis and cow parsley.*

ABOVE *When making designs for cuff-links, you may well be trying to achieve a plainer, more masculine effect. Try using grasses or heather against strong dark backgrounds.*

TOP RIGHT *With larger components still – these brooches are 1¹⁄₂ in (3.5 cm) high – it is possible to use even bigger flowers. (The two brooches at the top show astrantia (left) and larkspur (right).)*

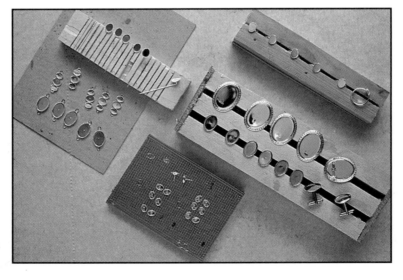

ABOVE *The pendant, stick pin, brooch and bangle all use the red bells of heuchera set against a white background to illustrate how effective this plain background can be in resin work.*

LEFT *A range of jewellery components with slightly upstanding edges to prevent the resin from flowing away. Flat components such as pendant or bangle cups present no problems, but levelling devices must be found for any components with projecting backs. The ear studs (foreground) are conveniently housed in a piece of stripboard, and the stick pins, rings, brooches and cufflinks are all slotted into wooden devices constructed especially for the purpose.*

cupboard 10 in (25 cm) wide × 12 in (30 cm) deep × 20 in (50 cm) high with three slatted shelves. It is thermostatically controlled by a fish-tank thermostat, and uses a 60W light bulb as a heater. It is coated inside with aluminium (aluminum) paint to reduce heat loss. This is a useful piece of equipment, but not essential. As an alternative, cure resin-work in a warm room (at least 70°F/

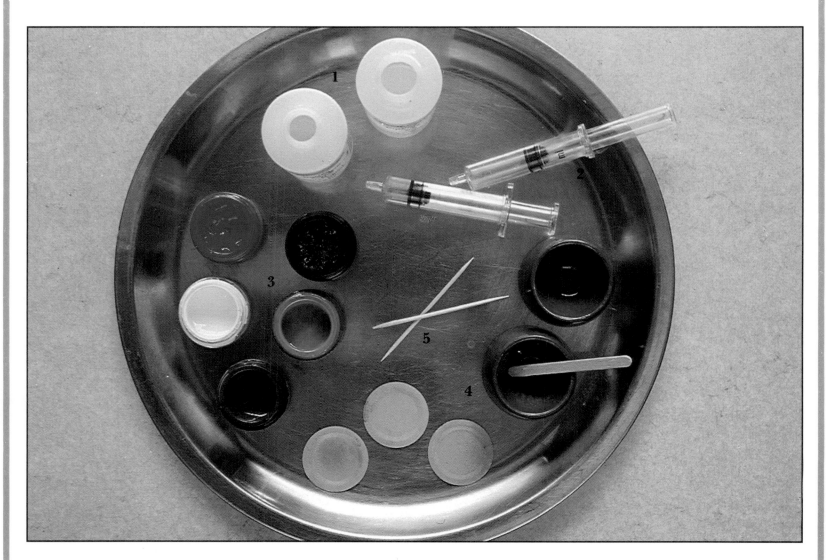

21°C) with a cardboard box over the item to protect it from dust.

PLANT MATERIAL

Plant material for use with resin should be gathered, pressed and stored in the normal way. Look for two particular characteristics: the flowers should be small (very small indeed for use in ear-studs and rings) and they should not lose their colour when set in resin. Experience will teach you which are the best flowers. In the meantime, I would suggest the following: for the tiniest items, use single flowers or buds of heuchera, forget-me-not or elderflower, or small groups of individual florets of cow parsley or astrantia. As the components increase in size a little, to include bangle-tops, pendants and cuff-links, you can, as well as using the flowers mentioned above, introduce slightly larger ones, like anaphalis (pearly everlasting), lobelia and heather. For bigger items like brooches add heartsease (wild pansy) and small larkspur to the selection.

Tiny leaves or small pieces of intricately-shaped foliage are also useful, as are both green and brown grasses. These are particularly suitable for cuff-links.

LEFT **Tools and equipment for resin work. 1** *Coating resin in two bottles for mixing together.* **2** *Hypodermic syringes for drawing off exact quantities of resin.* **3** *A series of colour pastes to create background colours.* **4** *Containers for mixing clear resin and small flat metal trays for mixing tiny quantities of coloured resin.* **5** *cocktail sticks for applying resin to components.*

LEFT *A curing cabinet for maintaining an even warm temperature and a dust-free atmosphere.*

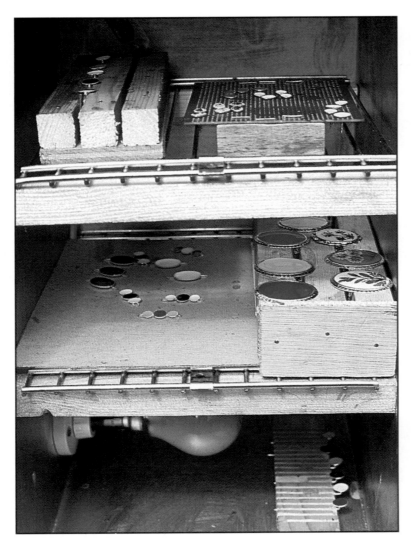

(Try using the smallest of the quaking grasses against a black background.) Do not forget delicate tendrils and stems – the fine red stems of heuchera look lovely with forget-me-nots.

I have been working with resin for only a relatively short period, but my experience so far suggests that if a flower is going to lose colour in resin, it will do so almost immediately. If, however, it keeps colour well at the start, it is likely to remain bright and I am therefore happy to use white backgrounds. A note of caution about darker backgrounds: whereas in conventional fabric-backed work, light flowers usually look good against dark backgrounds, take care when using pale flowers with any tendency towards translucency. Forget-me-nots, which look stunning against white, pink or pale blue, may well 'disappear' if you try to use them on a dark blue or black background.

PROCEDURE

APPLYING THE COLOURED BASE LAYER Measure exactly equal parts of the two resins into the mixing vessel. This is best done by pouring a small quantity from each bottle

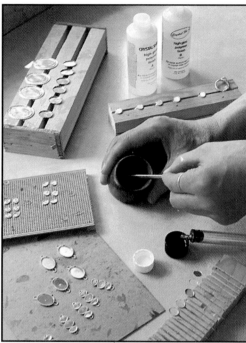
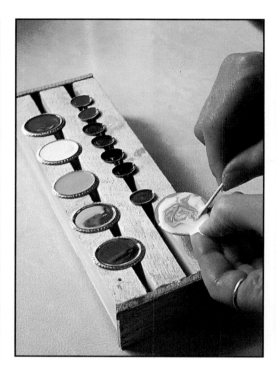

ABOVE ***Applying the coloured base layer 1*** *Draw off exact amounts of each type of resin using a different hypodermic syringe for each.*

ABOVE CENTRE *2 Stir thoroughly.*

into separate containers, and then using separate hypodermic syringes to draw off exact amounts. Only very small quantities are required, totalling no more than 2 tsp (10 ml), because the components are all small and the mix remains workable only for about 20 minutes.

Stir thoroughly for two to three minutes, making sure that the stirring stick comes into contact with the whole surface area of the container as well as with the fluid in its centre. Take care to lift the fluid from the bottom so that this too is blended.

Add colour paste in very small amounts until the background colour you want is attained. You can, of course, mix colours for a variety of effects. Lovely pale shades can be made by adding tiny amounts of red, green or royal blue to a basic white mix.

Ensure that the components are dust-free and lying completely flat.

Use a cocktail stick to apply a thin layer of resin in the required colour to the base of each item.

Allow this coat to cure for at least 24 hours in a curing cabinet or warm room before going on to the next stage.

MAKING THE FLOWER DESIGNS This is carried out in just the same way as for other miniature designs. Apply tiny amounts of glue to the back of the thickest part of each flower or leaf, and stick it to its coloured resin background. (Any unsecured item will float when the covering layer of resin is applied!)

APPLYING THE CLEAR COVERING LAYER Keep the designs in their levelling devices and repeat the measuring and

ABOVE *3 Add the colour paste in very small amounts. A tiny quantity of the royal blue paste is here being added to basic white mix to achieve an attractive pale blue.*

ABOVE *4 Use a cocktail stick to apply a thin layer of coloured resin to the base of each item.*

ABOVE CENTRE *The flower design is made in just the same way as when other backgrounds are used. Each item is stuck down with a tiny amount of glue.*

ABOVE *Apply the clear covering layer of resin with a cocktail stick.*

stirring steps as above, this time keeping the resin clear.

Use a cocktail stick, first to apply drops of resin to the design and then to make sure that the whole area is covered. Aim for a slightly convex finish. (The surface tension of the resin prevents the higher central part from flowing over the edges.) Even when the middle of a flower has been firmly glued down, it is possible that the outer edges of delicate petals may float upwards in the resin coating. This creates a very attractive three-dimensional effect and is no problem as long as the petal edges do not break through the surface of the resin.

It is important that this clear coating has a smooth finish and is bubble-free. If bubbles appear, help them to rise to the surface and burst by gently blowing or breathing on them. You might even apply a little heat from a hair-drier held some 10 in (25 cm) away from your work. Stubborn bubbles may respond only to being pierced with a pin.

Return designs to the curing cupboard for at least 24 hours. The resin cures fully in about a week.

MAKING RESIN PAPERWEIGHTS

If you enjoy working with resin, you may decide to try making larger items like the delightful paperweights illustrated.

The procedure for making such items is somewhat different from that outlined above. The flowers used here have not been pressed, but dried in their original three-dimensional form. This can be done by putting them in a plastic box containing a suitable desiccant, like borax or silica-gel – or, more traditionally, semolina

powder. The box should be closed and left in a warm, dry room for at least two weeks.

To make the paperweight, a small amount of clear polyester resin is poured into a plastic dish-shaped mould (mold). The flowers are then arranged, upside-down, in a first layer. As it begins to harden, a second, deeper layer is poured into the mould. (In larger designs a second layer of flowers may be embedded here.) The resin is then left to set hard around the flowers. The final step is to turn the paperweight out of the mould and apply a very thin layer of quick-setting resin to the base. This should be coloured to complement the flowers used.

I hope that the hints given above, together with the illustrations, have convinced you that working with resin is worth the trouble.

Warning: The resins referred to in this section are severe eye irritants and can be very harmful if swallowed. Care should be taken not to inhale the fumes; all such work should be carried out in a well-ventilated area. This is obviously not a suitable branch of the craft for children unless they are very closely supervised.

FRAMED PICTURES

The picture frame is the setting in which pressed-flower designs have traditionally been presented since they were first made. It is unlikely that anything will ever completely supplant this tried and trusted way of displaying flowers but, as in every other branch of the craft, modern materials, techniques and design ideas are beginning to have an influence.

Apart from the all-important flower designs, there are three elements to consider in relation to any larger framed picture: its background, its mount, if any, and its frame.

Whichever type of background you opt for, keep two objectives in mind. The first is to choose a colour and texture that enhance the overall effect of the design and frame. The second is to ensure that the background remains smooth and flat: if any unsightly ripples or wrinkles appear among the flowers, your design work will have been largely wasted.

CARD AND PAPER BACKGROUND

As we saw in Chapter 2, the simplest background to use is a piece of sturdy card, because the only preparation this needs is to be cut to size with a craft knife. Paper, on the other hand, may need to be glued to a stiffer background to ensure that it stays flat.

LEFT *An attractive paperweight made with 3-dimensional dried flowers set in embedding resin. The flowers used in the large design are scylla, candytuft, hesperis, alyssum and lobelia.*

ABOVE *Velvet should be prepared for use as a picture background by mounting it on a stiff backing card which is covered with a thin layer of latex adhesive.*

FABRIC BACKGROUND

This requires more careful preparation, but the extra effort should be worth while because of the variety of effects possible. The method of preparation depends on the nature of the selected fabric. Heavy materials like velvet are relatively easy to prepare: take a piece of stiff card which exactly fits the frame and cut the velvet to the same size; then cover the whole of one side of the card with a thin layer of latex adhesive, and, starting with a small area at the bottom of the card, smooth the fabric on to its background. If only a thin layer of adhesive is used, there is no danger of its showing through such thick fabric.

Unfortunately, the same cannot be said for finer fabrics like satin, for which an alternative way of ensuring a flat surface must be found. The method I recommend is as follows: cut a piece of stiff card to fit the frame, and some self-adhesive covering material to the same size; then cut the selected fabric to a slightly larger size; stick the covering carefully on to the fabric by the method described earlier in this chapter, leaving a regular border of about ½ in (1 cm) all round; then, using a latex adhesive, glue the uncovered edges of the fabric to the back of the stiff card. Start with the top edge and allow this to dry before sticking the bottom. This allows the fabric to be pulled taut and so ensures a good surface. When the bottom edge is dry, the two side edges may then be stuck one after the other.

MOUNTS

Strictly speaking, it is inadvisable to use a mount which prevents the flowers in a picture from touching the

ABOVE *Materials for preparing a satin background. 1 A piece of stiff card to fit the recess of the frame. 2 Self-adhesive covering cut to the same size and stuck onto a slightly larger piece of fabric.*
The next stage is to stick the uncovered edges to the back of the stiff card with a latex adhesive.

ABOVE RIGHT *When preparing a satin background for an oval frame, proceed as above but snip all round the uncovered edges of the satin so that it fits neatly around the oval shape.*

OPPOSITE ABOVE LEFT *Double mounts. Some effective combinations of top and base colours. Note the interesting effects that can be achieved by reversing their positions.*

OPPOSITE ABOVE RIGHT *Three designs on double mounts, based on heartsease, dog roses and larkspur. The small designs in the corners reflect the main design of each.*

A mountboard swatch showing the wide range of colours now available.

glass. I have already confessed to ignoring this advice with my fuchsia and larkspur 'trees' and have excused myself on the grounds that the flowers used in those designs are particularly sturdy and are therefore likely to survive unharmed. In general, however, I would not recommend the use of a cut-out mount for any more delicate flowers.

If you are unwilling to sacrifice this attractive method of presenting a picture, there are two ways round the problem. The first is to use a paper mount – which is so thin that it will hardly keep the flowers away from the glass (especially if a foam pad is used, as described in the framing section). The second, more interesting way round the problem is to use a special double mount.

These are a particularly attractive form of mount which were – as far as I know – designed specifically for use with pressed flowers. Each one is made in the normal way up to the point at which the inside oval or rectangle has been cut out. But then, instead of being discarded, the cut out piece is slightly reduced in size, and both pieces fixed to a plain rectangle of the same size but of a contrasting colour. The effect is unusual and pleasing, and the whole surface of the mount (except for the narrow contrasting border) makes contact with the glass, thus ensuring that any type of flower is kept in good condition.

This type of mount is very nearly as good as fabric for both subtlety of effect and versatility of use. There is now an amazing range of mountboard colours from which to choose, and it is immensely enjoyable to look through colour swatches to decide which combination of top and base colours will blend best with flowers, design and frame.

Because of the way these mounts are made, it is not essential to have a conventional frame. The outer part of the mount itself can act as a frame (especially if

Effective mirrors can be made by using single mounts and replacing the base board with mirror glass. I have used a bronze mirror for the brown montbretia design and the more usual silvered mirror glass for the blue larkspur design in the blue and silver frame.

decorated with small designs reflecting the larger one in the middle). The picture can then be protected by the use of a modern clip frame (see next section).

Simple rectangular mounts are easy to cut although bevelled edges take more practice. The accurate cutting of ovals requires more specialized equipment and should be done professionally.

MIRRORS

By way of a footnote on mounts, there is one excellent way of using a conventional cut-out mount while keeping the flowers perfectly pressed. This is to make a fairly elaborate design on the mount only, leaving the middle section, which does not touch the glass, without any flowers. This would normally look unsatisfactory – but not if the usual design background is replaced by a piece of mirror glass. This transforms the 'picture' into an attractive decorated mirror. Materials required are a frame and matching cut-out mount, a piece of ordinary picture glass, and a piece of mirror glass. It is sensible to protect the back of the whole assembly with a piece of card or thin hardboard.

ABOVE *If you decide to use a conventional frame with a double mount, there is ample opportunity for mixing and matching. The simple natural wood frame of the snowdrop picture enhances the natural simplicity of the design. The blue frame of the daisy picture matches the colour of the base mountboard which borders the oval design.*

FRAMES

The range of frames and mouldings (moldings) now available is so large that making a choice can occasionally be a bewildering process. Styles range from the traditional to the modern; the ornate to the plain; the wide and heavy to the slender and light. Frames may be rectangular, square, circular or oval. They may be made from wood, metal or plastic. There is an endless choice of colours, from antique gilts to gentle pastel shades, from the natural colours of wood to vivid modern hues.

The most satisfying way of choosing a frame is to take your work to a local picture-framer, so that you can actually select the most appropriate frame with your picture to hand. It is also, unfortunately, the most expensive. Other, cheaper, ways include buying a length of moulding (molding) and making a frame for yourself. (This should not be too difficult using a mitre block for cutting accurate corners.) Alternatively, before fixing on the exact size of the design background, you might decide on the style of the frame you want, and go out and buy a suitable one, ready-made. The picture can then be made to fit the frame.

ABOVE *A few of the many frames now available.*

The clip frames used in some of the pictures with the double mounts are relatively inexpensive and highly effective when used with any mounted picture. They consist simply of a piece of glass smoothed around the edges to prevent injury, and a piece of thick hardboard as backing. These are held together by four clips, the top one of which doubles as a hanging device. All that has to be done is to insert a mounted design between the glass and hardboard, and to clip the assembly together.

The least expensive, and sometimes the best, way of finding suitable frames is to keep your eyes open at second-hand sales. Old pictures are occasionally mounted in beautiful frames which may suit certain sorts of flower designs better than any modern frame could possibly do.

Glass

Picture glass is usually about $\frac{1}{16}$ in (0.2 cm) thick and comes either in the ordinary clear form, or as the non-reflective type. Decide which you prefer. Non-reflective glass is about double the price of its clear counterpart, but it does have the advantage of ensuring that any

ABOVE *Two lovely old frames acquired inexpensively in a sale.*

ABOVE *The components of a modern 'clip frame'.*

design should be clearly visible, wherever you hang it. A picture mounted on a dark background and glazed with ordinary glass will, if hung on a wall opposite a window, act as a mirror and you may well see more of yourself than of the picture! A second advantage of non-reflective glass is that it gives shiny fabrics like satin a lovely sparkling appearance.

ASSEMBLING A FRAMED FLOWER PICTURE

Unless you ask professionals to frame your work, you will need to know how to put a flower picture into a frame. First clean the glass carefully and fit it inside the frame, which should be placed, face downwards, on a soft surface (like a carpet or table-cloth); ensure that the completed flower design is free from any unwanted 'bits', and that each item is stuck down; place the design face down against the glass.

If the picture is fairly small ie a maximum of 9 in (23 cm) × 7 in (17 cm) and if the stiff backing on which it is mounted is sufficiently rigid, it may be perfectly satisfactory to fix it in place just as it is. If, however, the picture is larger, or the backing less rigid, you should

ABOVE *This wedding photograph shows the original bouquet from which the picture on the right was subsequently made.*

ding bouquet 'trademark' of two little holes through every rose petal and leaf.

Once it has served its decorative purpose, the bouquet should be dismantled and pressed as soon as possible. It can, if necessary, be kept fresh until the following morning by putting it carefully into a large plastic bag which is then inflated and sealed with a flexible tie. The bag should be stored in a cool place. The bottom of a refrigerator will do admirably, as long as there is no risk of petals being frozen. Do not be tempted, at any stage, to spray the flowers with water in an attempt to keep them fresh. This is distinctly unhelp-ful, for one of the aims in pressing flowers is to dry them out as quickly as possible.

In order to prepare the bouquet for pressing, carefully detach each flower and leaf from its wired stem and remove any staples from rosebuds. Select only the best specimens for pressing. The less perfect ones can be set aside, perhaps, for the preparation of a sweet-smelling *pot pourri*.

Some flowers need no preparation at all. Lily-of-

FAR RIGHT *The rose-coloured velvet background and the mahogany frame used for this bouquet picture blend with the flower colours and have a suitably 'traditional' feel.*

the-valley and heather, for example, can both be pressed just as they are, and gypsophila needs only to be divided into manageable sprays. Stephanotis (Madagascar jasmine) stems need separating into individual flowers, as do freesia, whose curving clusters of buds may, however, be pressed as a group. Other flowers – like roses, carnations and alstroemeria – must have each petal removed. Remember that the sepals of both roses and carnations should also be pressed for the later reconstruction of 'buds'.

The separate petals are delicate, so when using a press, remember to include additional sheets of blotting paper to prevent the corrugations of the card from imprinting themselves on the petals. You might alternatively prefer to press these specimens in a well weighted book. Roses and carnations are particularly prone to mildew, so it is a good idea to keep the press (or book) in a warm dry place for the first few days. All the flowers should be ready for use in about six weeks.

Remember when choosing a frame that because a bouquet normally consists of relatively large flowers, you really need a large design area. The oval frames illustrated measure 14 in (35 cm) × 11 in (27 cm).

Choose a background colour that both reflects the colour theme of the wedding and enhances the flowers. If the bride's and the bridesmaids' dresses have been specially made and there is any left over fabric, it may be possible to use this as background. But whatever the fabric used, it should be mounted on a stiff backing in one of the ways described in the earlier section on framed pictures.

Before beginning to work on the design it is necessary to make up reconstructions of both the buds and open flowers of roses and carnations and of 'new' alstroemeria flowers. (These will be quite different from the original, three-dimensional lily-like blooms, but with their lovely colour markings should be beautiful, nevertheless.)

There are many possible design shapes. The two that I think work best are those in the illustrations. The crescent-shaped design gracefully follows the curve of the frame, whereas the other one represents in two-dimensional form the original shape of the bouquet. (If you choose this second type of design, you will find that a photograph or a sketch is a helpful reminder of the shape you are attempting to recapture.)

You may also like to make some additional small designs in such settings as the little oval watch-top frames or hand-turned mahogany boxes, as souvenirs for bridesmaids, mothers and grandmothers. Design scope is naturally limited by the relatively large size of the flowers at your disposal, but like the main bouquet

picture they should each provide a lovely and lasting memento of a special day.

SPECIAL OCCASION PAPERWEIGHTS

There are many ways in which calligraphy can effectively be combined with flower designs. The examples illustrate one such combination which is very popular because it offers a way of making a gift for a special occasion just that little bit more personal.

A commemorative gift of this sort can be presented in almost any setting. All my examples are in oval paperweights, however, because I think the shape is well suited to calligraphy around the edge, and because the oval paperweights are ideal gifts for couples.

Plan the wording so that the inscription looks neither cramped nor unbalanced. Aunty Mary's paperweight has the maximum possible number of words. Alison's birthday gift has 18 on both sides for the sake of balance. Ada's name on the golden wedding presentation

is followed by a swung hyphen to balance it against the longer name of Albert.

The inscription can be written on the design card provided with the paperweight. The border left around the edge for writing should be in proportion to the design area. In order to mark it out, it is a good idea to make a template (which, in the case of these paperweights, should be about ¼ in (0.75 cm) smaller than the card all round.) Draw a faint pencil line round the template, and write the inscription outside this line. (If your handwriting is not up to the standard of your flower work, try to find somebody else to do it for you.)

Consider using a coloured ink which particularly suits the occasion, but unless you have chosen a dark background, be wary of silver and gold, for they do not always show up well.

Because the writing must obviously be done on paper or card, the whole process can be simplified by making the design directly on this background. When I am making a full and intricate design, through which the background will hardly show, I use this method, but I still prefer fabric for simpler designs.

The edge of the design area is clearly visible in this setting, so it is essential that fabric is backed with some self-adhesive covering film in order to prevent any unsightly fraying. The design oval can then be cut out, using the template described above. This must be done very carefully, for any slight irregularity of outline spoils the effect of the whole. Thick-piled material like velvet should be avoided: it would be almost impossible to achieve a good 'clean' edge with this. If there is some special reason to use a fabric that does not make a good edge, border it with something like the astrantia bracts used in the illustrated snowdrop paperweight. (This is a real example of making a virtue of necessity. The first time I did this it was simply because I was unhappy about a slightly ragged edge, but now I often choose this outline for simpler designs because it is so effective.)

It is a good idea to fix a fabric background into position using a good paper adhesive before beginning.

One of the delights of making these special occasion paperweights is matching flowers and the colours of design backgrounds to the occasion. I have already mentioned that I think the little violas, called heartsease

LEFT *A series of special occasion paperweights made to celebrate a variety of special occasions.*

ABOVE *An intricate design, celebrating the birth of a little boy.*

ABOVE *Suitable inscriptions are written around the edge of the card before the design is made (either on a fabric inset or directly onto the card).*

or wild pansy, together with heather, carry with them a lovely wish for a wedding day. I chose to use snowdrops to commemorate the birth of a little girl in winter; for a boy's birth I built up a very intricate and detailed design, mainly in strong blues and greens, highlighted with a little red. The ruby wedding anniversary is celebrated with the ruby-red 'blossom' of the heuchera 'tree'; and the golden wedding design is backed on golden satin. The two birthday designs were chosen because they were pretty and, in each case, suited the colour preference of their recipient.

Making these special occasion paperweights has probably given me more pleasure over the years than any other single area of my work, because I have enjoyed making designs to match occasions and have been pleased to hear how much people have enjoyed receiving them. But this, of course, is only one very small branch of the craft of flower pressing. It is my hope that, within the pages of this book, you will have found enough of interest to send you out into the sunshine to collect flowers for pressing at the first possible opportunity.

ACKNOWLEDGEMENTS

I would like to thank all those who have contributed designs to supplement my own work in providing the illustrations for this book. My thanks go first and foremost to Joan White for many of the designs in the purchased settings section; also to Jilly Ashby (symmetrical designs and landscapes); June Shippin (seed pictures); Doris Heaton (resin paperweights); Lily Grose (protected cards); Marjorie Gilbert (unprotected cards and book-marks and small mirror designs); Claire Blanshard (protected bookmarks); and my son Thomas who created many of the illustrations for the section on children's work.

I am grateful to two recent brides, Fiona Huggins and Nicola Swan, from whom I have 'borrowed back' the bouquet pictures; to Colin Mason of Potters Bar for the wedding photograph and to Brenda Smale for the bouquet; also to Rita Dizon for letting me hang on to the pictures which should have been delivered long ago.

My thanks are due to John Ellis, whose calligraphy adorns my special occasion paperweights, to Janice King and Julie Riley (Cooperative Extension Service, University of Alaska) for their helpful comments on North American flowers.

I acknowledge the loan of useful books from Keith Gray, Edna Godbold, Elsie Hart, Arthur Lloyd, Gus Peedo and Patricia Potter.

Finally, I should like to thank my daughter, Anna, for reading and commenting on the text, and my husband, Barry, for so productively using it as practice material while learning to use a word processor.

Index

Juliana (lily) 68
juniper *112*

K

key rings 215-6
kitchen towels 26
knives 10, *12,* 17
 use of 16, *16*

L

laburnum, fabric 118
lady's mantle *154,* 162, *162*
lampshades 210, *210*
larkspur 10, 15, *73,* 147, *154,* 158, 162, *162,* 174, *175,* 183, *183, 198, 204, 219,* 227, 288, *236*
latex adhesive 135
laurel leaves *91*
Leach, Bernard 18
lead crystal jars 220, 222
leaf prints 201, *202*
leaves, broad 17
Leguminosae 158
lemonade 17
lettuce 171
liatris *52, 60, 70*
 purple *34, 62*
lighting *47,* 54, 86
lilacs 16, *52, 58, 62,*69
lilies *69, 91,* 102, *103,* 156
 arum 26, *58, 70, 102*
 hybrid 68
 longiflorum *101,* 102
 white *101*
 yellow *101*
 see also arums

lily-of-the-valley *20,* 68, *20,* 68, *70, 90, 92,* 241, 242-3
Limnanthes 158, 174, *175*
 L. douglassii 161, *161*
Limonium sinuatum 165, *165*
line flowers 34
lobelia 154, 158, 163, *163, 204,* 205, *219,* 228
London pride 140, *140,* 141, 176
long-life powder *12*
loosestrife *78*
Lotus 44, 168, *168*
love-in-a-mist 140, *140,* 154, 163, *163,* 172, 173, *206, 216,* 219, *221*
lupins *75*
Lunaria annua 171

M

Madagascar jasmine *243*
magenta stock *61*
maidenhair fern 171
maple 170
 see also Acer
Maranta tricolor 87
marigolds 16, *77,* 171
masking foliage 41
meadow grass 171
meadow rue 169
mesh wire 24, *24,* 25, 26
Michaelmas daisies 67, 80
mildew 144, 243
miniatures, floral 116
minisecateurs *12*
minisecateurs *12*
mirrors 171, *210,* 211, 218, *219,* 236, *236*
misters 11, *12-3*
moisture *see* water
molucellas *41, 73, 74, 90*
 dried 117

monochromatic arrangements 52, *54,* 58, 62-3, *62-3*
montbretia 116, 136, *154,* 158, *158, 164, 176,* 199, *205, 216,* 221, *226*
moon daises 95
Moribana school 44
moss 24, *61, 86, 109, 116,* 119, 121, 142, 171
 reindeer 121
mounts 234-6, 237

N

Nagiere school 44
narcissi 69, 159, *159,* 223, *223*
Nephrolepis 87
Nephthytis 87
nettles *69*
Nigella damascena 163, *163*
 see also love-in-a-mist
nosegays 18, 92
nuts *112*

O

oak 170
Oasis-fix 10, *12, 24,* 26, *26,* 38
Oasis-prongs 38
Oasis-sec 121
Oasis-tape 11
orchids 156
Ottara school 44
orange 52
orchids 44
 Cymbidium 94
 Singapore 41, *95, 106*
oval arrangements 34